Workshop on Detecting Structure in Scholarly Discourse

(DSSD)

Held at the 50th Annual Meeting of the Association for Computational Linguistics (ACL 2012)

Jeju, Republic of Korea
12 July 2012

ISBN: 978-1-62748-346-9

Printed from e-media with permission by:

Curran Associates, Inc.
57 Morehouse Lane
Red Hook, NY 12571

Some format issues inherent in the e-media version may also appear in this print version.

Printed by Curran Associates, Inc. (2013)

Association for Computational Linguistics
209 N. Eighth Street
Stroudsburg, Pennsylvania 18360

Phone: 1-570-476-8006
Fax: 1-570-476-0860

acl@aclweb.org

Additional copies of this publication are available from:

Curran Associates, Inc.
57 Morehouse Lane
Red Hook, NY 12571 USA
Phone: 845-758-0400
Fax: 845-758-2634
Email: curran@proceedings.com
Web: www.proceedings.com

Preface

As this year is a celebration of the 50th ACL conference, we are delighted to be able to include the work presented in the first Workshop on Detecting Structure in Scholarly Discourse (DSSD) as part of these 50th anniversary proceedings.

Discourse structure, as a field of research within computational linguistics, is attracting renewed research interest, due to its increasing relevance to diverse fields such as bio-medical text analysis, ethnography, and scientific publishing. Much effort is directed at detecting and modeling a range of discourse elements at different levels of granularity and for different purposes. Such elements include: the statement of facts, claims, and hypotheses; the identification of methods and protocols; and the detection of novelty in contrast to the re-stating of previous existing work. More ambitious long-term goals include the modeling of argumentation, rhetorical structure, and narrative structure.

A broad variety of approaches and of features are used to identify discourse elements, including verb tense/mood/voice, semantic verb class, speculative language or negation, various classes of stance markers, text-structural components, or the location of references. The choice of features is often motivated by linguistic inquiry into the detection of subjectivity, opinion, entailment, inference, as well as author stance, author disagreement, motif and focus.

Six submissions were selected for presentation at the workshop. The submissions represent three fundamental perspectives of research concerning discourse structure: taxonomy and annotation, exploiting cross-document structure in text mining, and detecting discourse elements in scholarly texts. Further development of discourse models and of systems is likely to bring together and integrate aspects from all three. At the same time, these three perspectives give rise to interesting contrasts and different research questions, for instance: Are explicit taxonomies and annotation levels necessary for text mining and for the identification of particular types of discourse elements? or, more generally: How do these different perspectives all relate to a central theory of discourse? The workshop aims to be a forum for discussion of these exciting questions.

Along with our fellow workshop organizers Anita de Waard, Agnes Sandor, and Sophia Ananiadou, we would like to thank all the authors for the hard work that they put into their submissions. We are grateful to the members of the program committee for their thorough reviews. Special thanks go out to Eduard Hovy for his support, and to the ACL-2012 workshop co-chairs Massimo Poesio and Satoshi Sekine for their help with administrative matters. We also gratefully acknowledge the AMICUS (Automated Motif Discovery in Cultural Heritage and Scientific Communication Texts) network for endorsing and supporting the workshop.

Antal van den Bosch, Nijmegen, and Hagit Shatkay, Delaware
May 25, 2012

Organizers:

Sophia Ananiadou, School of Computer Science, University of Manchester, UK
Antal van den Bosch, Centre for Language Studies, Radboud University Nijmegen, The Netherlands
Ágnes Sándor, Xerox Research Europe, Grenoble, France
Hagit Shatkay, Dept. of Computer and Information Sciences, University of Delaware, USA
Anita de Waard, Elsevier Labs, USA

Program Committee:

Catherine Blake, University of Illinois at Urbana-Champaign, USA
Kevin Cohen, University of Colorado, USA
Nigel Collier, National Institute of Informatics, Japan
Walter Daelemans, University of Antwerp, Belgium
Robert Dale, Macquarie University, Australia
Kjersti Fløttum, University of Bergen, Norway
Rocana Girju, University of Illinois at Urbana-Champaign, USA
Lynette Hirschman, MITRE, USA
Halil Kilicoglu, Concordia University, Canada
Jin-Dong Kim, The University Of Tokyo, Japan
Anna Korhonen, Cambridge University, UK
Maria Liakata, Aberystwyth University, UK
Roser Morante, University of Antwerp, Belgium
Raheel Nawaz, University of Manchester, UK
Dragomir Radev, University of Michigan, USA
Dietrich Rebholz-Schuhmann, EBI, UK
Andrey Rzhetsky, University of Chicago, USA
Caroline Sporleder, Saarland University, Germany
Padmini Srinivasan, University of Iowa, USA
Simone Teufel, University of Cambridge, UK
Paul Thompson, University of Manchester, UK
Jun'ichi Tsujii, Microsoft Research Asia, China
Lucy Vanderwende, Microsoft Research, USA

Table of Contents

Conference Program

Thursday, July 12, 2012

Session 1: Exploiting Discourse Structure

9:00–9:45 *Identifying Comparative Claim Sentences in Full-Text Scientific Articles*
Dae Hoon Park and Catherine Blake

9:45–10:30 *Identifying Claimed Knowledge Updates in Biomedical Research Articles*
Ágnes Sándor and Anita de Waard

10:30–11:00 Coffee Break

Session 2: Detecting Discourse Elements

11:00–11:45 *Detection of Implicit Citations for Sentiment Detection*
Awais Athar and Simone Teufel

11:45–12:30 *Open-domain Anatomical Entity Mention Detection*
Tomoko Ohta, Sampo Pyysalo, Jun'ichi Tsujii and Sophia Ananiadou

12:30–2:00 Lunch

Session 3: Taxonomies and Annotation

2:00–2:45 *A Three-Way Perspective on Scientific Discourse Annotation for Knowledge Extraction*
Maria Liakata, Paul Thompson, Anita de Waard, Raheel Nawaz, Henk Pander Maat and Sophia Ananiadou

2:45–3:30 *Epistemic Modality and Knowledge Attribution in Scientific Discourse: A Taxonomy of Types and Overview of Features*
Anita de Waard and Henk Pander Maat

3:30–4:00 Coffee Break

4:00–5:00 Discussion between the authors on detecting and using discourse structure for scholarly text

5:00–5:30 Wrapup and close

Identifying Comparative Claim Sentences in Full-Text Scientific Articles

Dae Hoon Park[a]
[a]Department of Computer Science

University of Illinois at Urbana-Champaign
Urbana, IL 61801, USA
dpark34@illinois.edu

Catherine Blake[a,b]
[b]Center for Informatics Research in Science and Scholarship at the Graduate School of Library and Information Science
University of Illinois at Urbana-Champaign
Champaign, IL 61820-6211, USA
clblake@illinois.edu

Abstract

Comparisons play a critical role in scientific communication by allowing an author to situate their work in the context of earlier research problems, experimental approaches, and results. Our goal is to identify comparison claims automatically from full-text scientific articles. In this paper, we introduce a set of semantic and syntactic features that characterize a sentence and then demonstrate how those features can be used in three different classifiers: Naïve Bayes (NB), a Support Vector Machine (SVM) and a Bayesian network (BN). Experiments were conducted on 122 full-text toxicology articles containing 14,157 sentences, of which 1,735 (12.25%) were comparisons. Experiments show an F1 score of 0.71, 0.69, and 0.74 on the development set and 0.76, 0.65, and 0.74 on a validation set for the NB, SVM and BN, respectively.

1 Introduction

Comparisons provide a fundamental building block in human communication. We continually compare products, strategies, and political candidates in our daily life, but comparisons also play a central role in scientific discourse and it is not a surprise that comparisons appear in several models of scientific rhetoric. The Create a Research Space (CARS) model includes counter-claiming and establishing a gap during the 'establishing a niche' phase (Swales, 1990), and the Rhetorical Structure Theory includes a contrast schema and antithesis relation that is used between different nucleus and satellite clauses (Mann & Thompson, 1988). However, neither of these models identify where scientists make these comparisons. In contrast, Kircz's (1991) study of physics articles only mentions comparisons with respect to the use of data to compare with other experimental results (sections 4.3 and 8.1, respectively) with earlier work. Similarly, Teufel and Moen's contrast category (which includes the action lexicon s better_solution, comparison and contrast) is also restricted to contrasts with other work (Teufel & Moens, 2002). Lastly the Claim Framework (CF) includes a comparison category, but in contrast to the earlier comparisons that reflect how science is situated within earlier work, the CF captures comparisons between entities (Blake, 2010).

Identifying comparisons automatically is difficult from a computational perspective (Friedman, 1989). For example, the following sentence is not a comparison even though it contains two words (more than) which are indicative of comparisons. *More than five methods were used.* Bresnan claimed that 'comparative clause construction in English is almost notorious for its syntactic complexity' (Bresnan, 1973), p275. Perhaps due to this complexity, several instructional books have been written to teach such constructs to non-native speakers.

Our goal in this paper is to automatically identify comparison claims from full-text scientific articles, which were first defined in Blake's Claim Framework (Blake, 2010). Comparisons capture a binary relationship between two concepts within a sentence and the aspect on which the comparison is made. For example, 'patients with AML' (a type of leukemia) and 'normal controls' are being compared in the following sentence, and the aspect on which the comparison is made is 'the plasma concentration of nm23-H1'. *The plasma concentration of nm23-H1 was higher in patients with AML than in normal controls (P = .0001).* In this paper, we focus on identifying comparison sentences and leave extraction of the two concepts and the aspect on which the comparison is made as future work. Similar to earlier comparison sentences in biomedicine, we consider the sentence as the unit of analysis (Fiszman, et al, 2007).

To achieve this goal, we cast the problem as a classification activity and defined both semantic and syntactic features that are indicative of comparisons based on comparison sentences that were kindly provided by Fiszman (2007) and Blake (2010). With the features in place, we conducted experiments using the Naïve Bayes (NB) and Support Vector Machine (SVM) classifiers, which both work well on text. We then introduce a Bayesian Network (BN) that removes some of the independence assumptions made in NB model. The subsequent evaluation considers more than 1,735 comparison claim sentences that were identified in 122 full text toxicology articles.

Although automatically detecting comparison sentences in full-text articles is challenging, we believe that the information conveyed from such sentences will provide a powerful new way to organize scientific findings. For example, a student or researcher could enter a concept of interest and the system would provide all the comparisons that had been made. Such a system would advance our general knowledge of information organization by revealing what concepts *can* be compared. Such a strategy could also be used for query expansion in information retrieval, and comparisons have already been used for question answering (Ballard, 1989).

2 Related Work

Comparisons play an important role in models of scientific discourse (see Introduction), because authors can compare research hypotheses, data collection methods, subject groups, and findings. Comparisons are similar to the antithesis in the CARS model (Swales, 1990), the contrast schema in RST (Mann & Thompson, 1988) and in (Teufel & Moens, 2002) and the comparisons category of the CF model (Blake, 2010).

From a computational linguistic perspective, Bresnan (1973) described the comparative clause construction in English as 'almost notorious for its syntactic complexity'. Friedman (1989) also pointed out that comparative structure is very difficult to process by computer since comparison can occur in a variety of forms pervasively throughout the grammar and can occur almost anywhere in a sentence. In contrast to the syntax description of comparison sentences, Staab and Hahn (1997) provided a description logic representation of comparative sentences. Each of these linguists studied the construction of comparative sentence, but did not distinguish comparatives from non-comparative sentences.

Beyond the linguistic community, Jindal and Liu (2006) have explored comparisons between products and proposed a comparative sentence mining method based on sequential rule mining with words and the neighboring words' Part-of-Speech tags. The sequential rules are then used as features in machine learning algorithms. They report that their method achieved a precision of 79% and a recall of 81% on their data set. We too frame the problem as a classification activity, but Jindal and Liu use Part-of-Speech tags and indicator words as features while we use a dependency tree representation to capture sentence features. We also constructed a Bayesian Network to remove the independence assumption of Naïve Bayes classifier. The comparison definition used here also reflects the work of Jindal and Liu (2006).

The work on product review comparisons was subsequently extended to identify the preferred product; for example, camera X would be extracted from the sentence "*the picture quality of Camera X is better than that of Camera Y.*" (Ganapathibhotla and Liu, 2008). Features used for this subsequent work included a comparative word, compared features, compared entities, and a comparison type. Most recently, Xu et al. (2011) explored comparative opinion mining using Conditional Random Fields (CRF) to identify different types of comparison relations where two product names must be present in a sentence. They report that their approach achieved a higher F1 score than the Jindal and Liu's method on mobile phone review data.

Yang and Ko (2011) used maximum entropy method and Support Vector Machines (SVM) to identify comparison sentences from the web based on keywords and Part-of-Speech tags of their neighboring words. They achieved an F1-score of 90% on a data set written in Korean.

The experiments reported here consider articles in biomedicine and toxicology which are similar to those used by Fiszman et al. who identified comparisons between drugs reported in published clinical trial abstracts (Fiszman et al., 2007). However, their definition of comparative sentence is narrower than ours in that non-gradable comparative sentences are not considered. Also, the goal is to classify type of comparative sentences which is different from identifying comparative sentences from a full-text article that contains non-comparative sentences as well.

From a methodological standpoint, Naïve Bayes (NB), Support Vector Machines (SVM), and Bayesian Network (BN) have been explored for variety of text classification problems (Sebastiani, 2002). However, we are not aware of any studies that have explored these methods to identify comparison sentences in full-text scientific articles.

3 Method

Our goal is to automatically identify comparison sentences from full text articles, which can be framed as a classification problem. This section provides the definitions used in this paper, a description of the semantic and syntactic features, and the classifiers used to achieve the goal. Stated formally: Let $S = \{S_1, S_2, \ldots, S_N\}$ be a set of sentences in a collection D. The features extracted automatically from those sentences will be $X = \{X_1, X_2, \ldots, X_M\}$. Each feature X_j is a discrete random variable and has a value X_{ij} for each sentence S_i. Let C_i be a class variable that indicates whether a sentence S_i is a comparative. Thus, the classifier will predict C_i based on the feature values $X_{i1}, X_{i2}, \ldots, X_{iM}$ of S_i.

3.1 Definitions

A ***comparative sentence*** describes at least one similarity or difference relation between two entities. The definition is similar to that in (Jindal & Liu, 2006). A sentence may include more than one comparison relation and may also include an aspect on which the comparison is made. We require that the entities participating in the comparison relation should be non-numeric and exist in the same sentence.

A ***comparison word*** expresses comparative relation between entities. Common comparison words include 'similar', 'different', and adjectives with an '-er' suffix. A ***compared entity*** is an object in a sentence that is being compared with another object. Objects are typically noun phrases, such as a chemical name or biological entity. Other than being non-numeric, no other constraints apply to the compared entities. A ***compared aspect*** captures the aspect on which two comparison entities are compared. The definition is similar to a *feature* in (Jindal & Liu, 2006). For example: *the level of significance differed greatly between the first and second studies*. A compared aspect is optional in comparative sentence.

There are two comparative relation types: *gradable* and *non-gradable* (Jindal & Liu, 2006), and we further partition the latter into non-gradable similarity comparison and non-gradable difference comparison. Also, we consider equative comparison (Jindal & Liu, 2006) as non-gradable. ***Gradable comparisons*** express an ordering of entities with regard to a certain aspect. For example, sentences with phrases such as 'greater than', 'decreased compared with', or 'shorter length than' are typically categorized into this type. The sentence "*The number of deaths was higher for rats treated with the Emulphor vehicle than with corn oil and increased with dose for both vehicles*" is a gradable difference comparison where *'higher'* is a comparison word, *'rats treated with the Emulphor vehicle'* and *'rats treated with corn oil'* are compared entities, and *'the number of deaths'* is a compared aspect.

Non-gradable similarity comparisons state the similarity between entities. Due to nature of similarity, it has a non-gradable property. Phrases such as 'similar to', 'the same as', 'as ~ as', and 'similarly' can indicate similarity comparison in the sentence. The sentence "*Mean maternal body weight was similar between controls and treated groups just prior to the beginning of dosing.*" is an example of similarity comparison where *'similar'* is a comparison word, *'controls'* and *'treated* *groups'* are compared entities, and *'Mean maternal body weight'* is a compared aspect.

Non-gradable difference comparisons express the difference between entities without stating the order of the entities. For example, comparison phrases such as 'different from' and 'difference between' are present in non-gradable difference comparison sentences. In the sentence "*Body weight gain and food consumption were not significantly different between groups*" there is a single term entity 'groups', and a comparison word 'different'. With the entity and comparison word, this sentence has two comparative relations: one with a compared aspect 'body weight gain' and another with 'food consumption'.

3.2 Feature representations

Feature selection can have significant impact on classification performance (Mitchell, 1997). We identified candidate features in a pilot study that considered 274 comparison sentences in abstracts (Fiszman et al., 2007) and 164 comparison claim sentences in full text articles (Blake, 2010). Thirty-five features were developed that reflect both lexical and syntactic characteristics of a sentence. Lexical features explored in these experiments include:

L1: The first lexical feature uses terms from the SPECIALIST lexicon (Browne, McCray, & Srinivasan, 2000), a component of the Unified Medical Language System (UMLS[1], 2011AB) and is set to true when the sentence contains any inflections that are marked as comparisons. We modified the lexicon by adding terms in {'better', 'more', 'less', 'worse', 'fewer', 'lesser'} and removing terms in {'few', 'good', 'ill', 'later', 'long-term', 'low-dose', 'number', 'well', 'well-defined'}, resulting in 968 terms in total.

L2: The second lexical feature captures direction. A lexicon of 104 words was created using 82 of 174 direction verbs in (Blake, 2010) and an additional 22 manually compiled words. Selections of direction words were based on how well the individual word predicted a comparison sentence in the development set. This feature is set to true when a sentence contains any words in the lexicon.

[1] http://www.nlm.nih.gov/research/umls/quickstart.html

L3: Set to true when a sentence includes any of the following words: *from, over* or *above.*

L4: Set to true when the sentence includes either *versus* or *vs.*

L5: Set to true when the sentence includes the phrase *twice the.*

L6: Set to true when the sentence includes any of the following phrases *times that of, half that of, third that of, fourth that of*

The 27 syntactic features use a combination of semantics (words) and syntax. Figure 1 shows a dependency tree that was generated using the Stanford Parser (version 1.6.9) (Klein & Manning, 2003). The tree shown in Figure 1 would be represented as:

ROOT [*root* orders [*nsubj* DBP, *cop* is, *amod* several, *prep* of [*pobj* magnitude [*amod* mutagenic/carcinogenic [*advmod* more], *prep* than [*pobj* BP]], *punct* .]]

where dependencies are shown in italics and the tree hierarchy is captured using []. The word ROOT depicts the parent node of the tree.

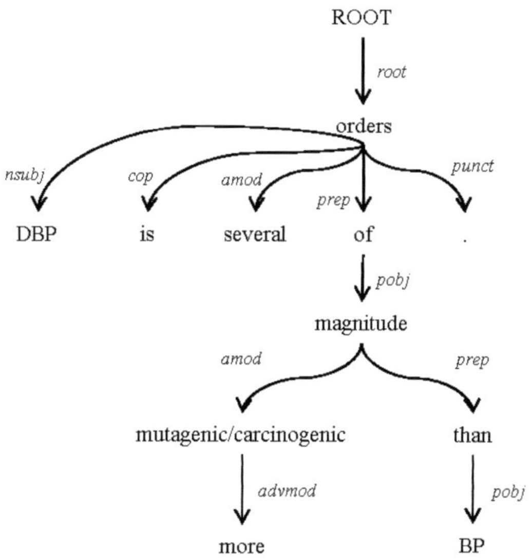

Figure 1. Dependency tree for the sentence *"DBP is several orders of magnitude more mutagenic/carcinogenic than BP."*

We compiled a similarity and difference lexicon (*SIMDIF*), which includes 31 words such as *similar*, *different*, and *same*. Words were selected in the same way as the direction words (see L2). Each term in the *SIMDIF* lexicon has a corresponding set of prepositions that were collected from dictionaries. For example, the word *different* in the *SIMDIF* lexicon has two corresponding prepositions: 'from' and 'than'.

The first four syntactic rules capture comparisons containing words in *SIMDIF,* and rules 5 through 24 capture comparisons related to the features L1, L2, or both. Each of the rules 25 and 26 consists of a comparative phrase and its syntactic dependency. Each rule is reflected as a Boolean feature that is set to true when the rule applies and false otherwise. For example, rule S1 would be true for the sentence "X is similar to Y".

Subscripts in the templates below depict the word identifier and constraints applied to a word. For example W_{2_than} means that word 2 is drawn from the domain of (than), where numeric values such as 2 are used to distinguish between words. Similarly, W_{4_SIMDIF} means that the word 4 is drawn from terms in the *SIMDIF* lexicon. The symbols |, ¬, ?, and * depict disjunctions, negations, optional, and wildcard operators respectively.

S1: [*root* W_{1_SIMDIF} [*nsubj|cop* W_2, (*prep* W_3)?]]
S2: [¬*root* W_{1_SIMDIF} [*nsubj|cop* W_2, (*prep* W_3)?]]

Syntactic rules 3 and 4 capture other forms of non-gradable comparisons with connected prepositions.

S3: [(prep W_1)?, (* W_2)? [(*prep* W_3)?, (*acomp|nsubjpass|nsubj|dobj|conj*) W_{4_SIMDIF} [(*prep* W_5)?]]]
S4: [(prep W_1)?, (* W_2)? [(*prep* W_3)?, ¬(*acomp|nsubjpass|nsubj|dobj|conj*) W_{4_SIMDIF} [(*prep* W_5)?]]]

The following syntactic rules capture other non-gradable comparisons and gradable comparisons. For example, the comparative sentence example in Figure 1 has the component [*prep* than], which is satisfied by rule S5. One additional rule (rule **S27**) uses a construct of 'as … as', but it's not included here due to space limitations.

S5: [*prep* W_{1_than}]
S6: [*advmod* W_{1_than}]
S7: [*quantmod|mwe* W_{1_than}]
S8: [*mark* W_{1_than}]
S9: [*dep* W_{1_than}]
S10: [¬(*prep|advmod|quantmod|mwe|mark|dep)* W_{1_than}]
S11: [*advcl|prep* $W_{1\_compared}$]
S12: [*dep* $W_{1\_compared}$]
S13: [¬ *(advcl|prep|dep)* $W_{1\_compared}$]
S14: [*advcl* $W_{1\_comparing}$]
S15: [*partmod|xcomp* $W_{1\_comparing}$]
S16: [*pcomp* $W_{1\_comparing}$]
S17: [*nsubj* $W_{1\_comparison}$]
S18: [*pobj* $W_{1\_comparison}$]
S19: [¬ *(nsubj|pobj)* $W_{1\_comparison}$]
S20: [*dep* $W_{1\_contrast}$]
S21: [*pobj* $W_{1\_contrast}$]
S22: [*advmod* $W_{1\_relative}$]
S23: [*amod* $W_{1\_relative}$]
S24: [¬*(advmod|amod)* $W_{1\_relative}$]
S25: $W_{1\_compare}$ [*advmod* $W_{2\_(well|favorably)}$]
S26: $W_{1\_\%}$ [*nsubj* W_2 [*prep* W_{3_of}]]

Two additional general features were used. The preposition feature (*PREP*) captures the most indicative preposition among connected prepositions in the rules 1 through 4. It is a nominal variable with six possible values, and the value assignment is shown in Table 1. When more than two values are satisfied, the lowest value is assigned. The plural feature (*PLURAL*) for the rules 1 through 4 is set to true when the subject of a comparison is in the plural form and false otherwise. These two features provide information on if the sentence contains compared entities which are required in a comparison sentence.

Value	Preposition connected to *SIMDIF* word
1	*between*, *among*, or *across*
2	proper preposition provided in *SIMDIF*
3	*between*, *among*, or *across*, but may not be connected to *SIMDIF* word
4	*in* or *for*
5	any other prepositions or no preposition
6	no *SIMDIF* word is found

Table 1: *PREP* value assignment

3.3 Classifiers

The Naïve Bayes (NB), Support Vector Machine (SVM) and Bayesian Network (BN) classifiers were used in these experiments because they work well with text (Sebastiani, 2002).

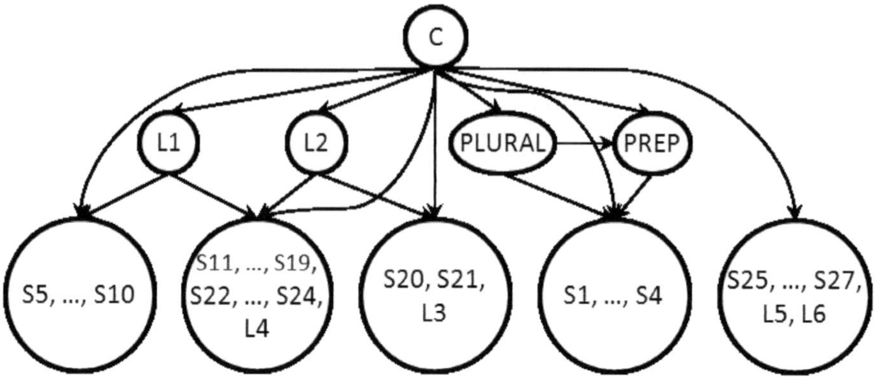

Figure 2: Bayesian Network for comparative sentences. Multiple features having the same connections are placed in a big circle node for the purpose of simple representation. C is a class variable (comparative).

The Bayesian Network model was developed to remove the independence assumption in the NB model. BN is a directed acyclic graph that can compactly represent a probability distribution because only the conditional probabilities (rather than the joint probabilities) need to be maintained. Each node in the BN represents a random variable X_i and each directed edge reflects influence from the parent node to the child node.

In order to improve Naïve Bayes classifier, we designed our Bayesian Network model by capturing proper conditional dependencies among features. Figure 2 shows the BN model used in our experiments. The relationships between features in BN were determined heuristically. Based on our observation, most gradable comparisons contain both comparison words and corresponding prepositions, so we connected such pairs. Also, most non-gradable comparisons contained comparison words and different kinds of prepositions depending on syntactic structure and plurality of subjects, and these relations are captured in the network. For example, features S5 through S10 depend on L1 because a preposition 'than' can be a good indicative word only if there is a comparison word of L1 in the same sentence. Parameters for the BN were estimated using maximum likelihood estimation (MLE) with additive smoothing. Exact inference is feasible because all nodes except for the class node are observed.

4 Results and Discussion

A pilot study was conducted using 297 and 165 sentences provided by (Fiszman et al., 2007) and (Blake, 2010) respectively to identify an initial set of features. Features were then refined based on the development set described below (section 3 reports the revised features). The BN model was also created based on results in the development set.

Sentence Type	Development	Validation
Comparative Sentences	1659 (12.15%)	76 (15.2%)
Non-comparative sentences	11998 (87.85%)	424 (84.8%)
Total	13657 (100%)	500 (100%)

Table 2: Distribution of comparative and non-comparative sentences.

Experiments reported in this paper consider 122 full text articles on toxicology. Figures, tables, citations, and references were removed from the corpus, and a development set comprising 83 articles were drawn at random which included 13,657 headings and sentences (the *development set).* Articles in the development set were manually inspected by three annotators to identify comparison claim sentences. Annotators met weekly to discuss problematic sentences and all comparison sentences were subsequently reviewed by the first author and updated where required to ensure consistency. Once the feature refinements and BN were complete, a random sample of 500 sentences was drawn from the remaining 39 articles (the *validation set*) which were then annotated by the first author. Table 2 shows that the number of comparison and non-comparison sentences are similar between the development and validation sets.

The NB, SVM (LIBSVM package), and BN implementations from WEKA were used with their default settings (Hall et al., 2009; Chang and Lin, 2011). Classifier performance was measured using stratified 10-fold cross validation and a paired t-test was performed (using two-tail p-values 0.05 and 0.01) to determine if the performance of the BN model was significantly different from the NB and SVM.

We measured accuracy, the proportion of correct predictions, and the area under a ROC curve (ROC AUC), which is a plot of true positive rate vs. false positive rate. Given the skewed dataset (only 12% of the development sentences are comparisons), we recorded precision, recall, and F1 score of each class, where F1 score is a harmonic mean of precision and recall.

	NB	SVM	BN
Accuracy	0.923	0.933	$\mathbf{0.940}^{++}_{++}$
ROC AUC	0.928	0.904	$\mathbf{0.933}^{++}_{++}$
Comp. Precision	0.653	0.780	$\mathbf{0.782}^{++}$
Comp. Recall	**0.778**	0.621	0.706^{--}_{++}
Comp. F1 score	0.710	0.691	$\mathbf{0.742}^{++}_{++}$
Non-comp. Precision	**0.968**	0.949	0.960^{--}_{++}
Non-comp. Recall	0.943	**0.976**	0.973^{++}_{-}
Non-comp. F1 score	0.955	0.962	$\mathbf{0.966}^{++}_{++}$

Table 3: Development set results. Superscripts and subscripts depict statistical significance for BN vs. NB and BN vs. SVM respectively. +/- is significant at p=0.05 and ++/-- is significant at p=0.01. Bold depicts the best performance for each metric.

Table 3 shows the development set results. The accuracy and area under the ROC curve was significantly higher in BN compared to the NB and SVM models. For comparative sentences, recall was the highest with NB, but F1 score was significantly higher with BN. Although the difference was small, the F1 score for non-comparative sentences was significantly highest in the BN model.

Table 4 shows the validation set results, which are similar to the development set in that the BN model also achieved the highest accuracy and area under the ROC curve. The BN model had the highest non-comparative F1 score, but NB had a higher F1 score on comparatives.

	NB	SVM	BN
Accuracy	0.924	0.916	**0.932**
ROC AUC	0.948	0.883	**0.958**
Comp. Precision	0.726	**0.886**	0.875
Comp. Recall	**0.803**	0.513	0.645
Comp. F1 score	**0.763**	0.650	0.742
Non-comp. Precision	**0.964**	0.919	0.939
Non-comp. Recall	0.946	**0.988**	0.983
Non-comp. F1 score	0.955	0.952	**0.961**

Table 4: Validation set results.

The results suggest that capturing dependencies between features helped to improve the BN performance in some cases. For example, unlike the BN, the NB and SVM models incorrectly classified the following sentence as comparative: "*The method of <u>forward</u> <u>difference</u> was selected for calculation of sensitivity coefficients.*" The words 'forward' and 'difference' would activate features L2 and S4, respectively, and 5 would be assigned for PREP. Since the BN model captures dependencies between L and S features and between S and the PREP feature, the probability in the BN model would not increase as much as in the NB model. To better understand the features, we conducted an error analysis of the BN classifier on validation set (see Table 5).

		Predicted	
	Class	0	1
Actual	Non-comparative (0)	417	7
	Comparative (1)	27	49

Table 5. Validation confusion matrix for BN.

We conducted a closer inspection of the seven false positives (i.e. the non-comparative sentences that were predicted comparative). In four cases, sentences were predicted as comparative because two or more independent weak features were true. For example, in the sentence below, the features related to 'compared' (rule S11) and 'different' (rule S4) were true and produced an incorrect classification. "*Although these data cannot be compared directly to those in the current study because they are in a different strain of rat (Charles River CD), they clearly illustrate the variability in the incidence of glial cell tumors in rats.*" This sentence is not comparative for *compared* since there is no comparison word between *these data* and *current study*. Similarly, this sentence is not comparative for *different* since only one *compared entity* is present for it.

Two of the remaining false positive sentences were misclassified because the sentence had a comparison word and comparison entities, but the sentence was not a *claim*. The last incorrect sentence included a comparison with a numeric value.

Reason of misclassification	# errors
Probability is estimated poorly	10
Comparison is partially covered by dependency features	7
Comparison word is not in lexicon	7
Dependency parse error	3
Total	27

Table 6. Summary of false negative errors.

We also investigated false negatives (i.e. comparative sentences that were predicted as non-comparative by the BN). The reasons of errors are summarized in Table 6. Out of 27 errors, poor estimation was responsible for ten errors. These errors mostly come from the sparse feature space. For example, in the sentence below, the features related to 'increased' (rule L2) and 'comparison' (rule S18) were active, but the probability of comparison is 0.424 since the feature space of 'comparison' feature is sparse, and the feature is not indicative enough. "*Mesotheliomas of the testicular tunic were statistically (p < 0.001) increased in the high-dose male group in comparison to the combined control groups.*"

Seven of the false negative errors were caused by poor dependency features. In this case, the comparison was covered by either the parent or the child feature node, not by both. Other seven errors were caused by missing terms in the lexicons, and the last three were caused by a dependency parse error.

5 Conclusion

Comparison sentences play a critical role in scientific discourse as they enable an author to fully engage the reader by relating work to earlier research hypotheses, data collection methods, subject groups, and findings. A review scientific discourse models reveals that comparisons have been reported as the thesis/antithesis in CARS (Swales, 1990), the contrast category in RST (Mann & Thompson, 1988) in Teufel & Moens (2002) and as a comparisons category in CF (Blake, 2010).

In this paper, we introduce 35 features that capture both semantic and syntactic characteristics of a sentence. We then use those features with three different classifiers, Naïve Bayes, Support Vector Machines, and Bayesian Networks to predict comparison sentences. Experiments consider 122 full text documents and 14,157 sentences, of which 1,735 express at least one comparison. To our knowledge, this is the largest experiment on comparison sentences expressed in full-text scientific articles.

Results show that the accuracy and F1 scores of the BN were statistically ($p<=0.05$) higher than those of both the NB and SVM classifiers. Results also suggest that scientists report claims using a comparison sentence in 12.24% of the full-text sentences, which is consistent with, but more prevalent than in an earlier Claim Framework study which reported a rate of 5.11%. Further work is required to understand the source of this variation and the degree to which the comparison features and classifiers used in this paper can also be used to capture comparisons of scientific papers in other domains.

Acknowledgement

This material is based upon work supported by the National Science Foundation under Grant No. (1115774). Any opinions, findings, and conclusions or recommendations expressed in this material are those of the author(s) and do not necessarily reflect the views of the National Science Foundation.

References

Ballard, B.W. (1989). A General Computational Treatment of Comparatives for Natural Language Question Answering, Association of Computational Linguistics. Vancouver, British Columbia, Canada.

Blake, C. (2010). Beyond genes, proteins, and abstracts: Identifying scientific claims from full-text biomedical articles. Journal of Biomedical Informatics, 43, 173-189.

Bresnan, J.W. (1973). Syntax of the Comparative Clause Construction in English. Linguistic Inquiry, 4(3), 275-343.

Chih-Chung Chang and Chih-Jen Lin, LIBSVM : a library for support vector machines. ACM Transactions on Intelligent Systems and Technology, 2:27:1--27:27, 2011.

Browne, A.C., McCray, A.T., & Srinivasan, S. (2000). The SPECIALIST LEXICON. Bethesda, Maryland.

Fiszman, M., Demner-Fushman, D., Lang, F.M., Goetz, P., & Rindflesch, T.C. (2007). In Interpreting Comparative Constructions in Biomedical Text. (pp. 37-144).

Friedman, C. (1989). A General Computational Treatment Of The Comparative, Association of Computational Linguistics (pp. 161-168). Stroudsburg, PA.

Ganapathibhotla, M., & Liu, B. (2008). Mining Opinions in Comparative Sentences. International Conference on Computational Linguistics (Coling). Manchester, UK.

Hall, M., Frank, E., Holmes, G., Pfahringer, B., Reutemann, P., & Witten, I.H. (2009). The WEKA Data Mining Software: An Update. SIGKDD Explorations, 11(1).

Jindal, N., & Liu, B. (2006). Identifying Comparative Sentences in Text Documents, Special Interest Group in Information Retrieval (SIGIR) Seattle Washington USA, 244-251.

Jindal, N., & Liu, B. (2006). Mining Comparative Sentences and Relations, American Association for Artificial Intelligence Boston, MA.

Kircz, J.G. (1991). Rhetorical structure of scientific articles: the case for argumentation analysis in information retrieval. Journal of Documentation, 47(4), 354-372.

Klein, D., & Manning, C.D. (2003). In Fast Exact Inference with a Factored Model for Natural Language Parsing. Advances in Neural Information Processing Systems, 3-10.

Mann, W.C., & Thompson, S.A. (1988). Rhetorical Structure Theory: Toward a Functional Theory of Text Organization. Text, 8(3), 243-281.

Mitchell, T.M. (1997). Machine Learning: McGraw-Hill.

Sebastiani, F. (2002). Machine learning in automated text categorization. ACM Computing Surveys, 34(1), 1 - 47.

Staab, S., & Hahn, U. (1997). Comparatives in Context. National Conference on AI. National Conference on Artificial Intelligence 616-621.

Swales, J. (1990). Genre Analysis: English in Academic and Research Settings: Cambridge Applied Linguistics.

Teufel, S., & Moens, M. (2002). Summarizing Scientific Articles -- Experiments with Relevance and Rhetorical Status. Computational Linguistics, 28(4), 409-445.

Xu, K., Liao, S., Li, J., & Song, Y. (2011). Mining Comparative Opinions from Customer Reviews for Competitive Intelligence. Decision Support Systems, 50(4), 743-754.

Yang, S., & Ko, Y. (2011). Extracting Comparative Entities and Predicates from Texts Using Comparative Type Classification, Association of Computation Linguistics. Portland, OR.

Identifying Claimed Knowledge Updates in Biomedical Research Articles

Ágnes Sándor
Xerox Research Centre Europe
Agnes.Sandor@xrce.xerox.com

Anita de Waard
Elsevier Labs, USA
A.Dewaard@elsevier.com

Abstract

Key knowledge components of biological research papers are conveyed by structurally and rhetorically salient sentences that summarize the main findings of a particular experiment. In this article we define such sentences as Claimed Knowledge Updates (CKUs), and propose using them in text mining tasks. We provide evidence that CKUs convey the most important new factual information, and thus demonstrate that rhetorical salience is a systematic discourse structure indicator in biology articles along with structural salience. We assume that CKUs can be detected automatically with state-of-the-art text analysis tools, and suggest some applications for presenting CKUs in knowledge bases and scientific browsing interfaces.

1 Introduction

Biomedical research articles describe newly discovered biological findings, and in doing so, update the readers' knowledge on a particular topic. These two functions of research articles – describing reality and updating knowledge in a field – mobilize different forms of linguistic expression: on the one hand, in order to describe pieces of reality, the authors refer to biological objects and relationships among them, and on the other hand, they shape the way in which new knowledge is inserted into existing accumulated knowledge, through argumentation, discourse and rhetorical structure. The designers of text mining systems are increasingly aware of the importance of integrating both aspects into annotation schemes, and thus models of argumentation, discourse and rhetorical structure are becoming integrated with models of biological reality in modern annotation systems, such as described in Liakata et al. (2010), Nawaz et al. (2010), Wilbur et al. (2006), Sándor (2007), Teufel (1999) and Collier (2006).

Models of biological knowledge are commonly mapped to well-defined linguistic elements like named entities (mostly noun phrases), relationships between the entities (mostly predicates), and these are reliably detected with state-of-the-art text-mining tools (e.g., Nawaz et al. 2010). But the detection of argumentation, discourse and rhetorical structures, and the association of linguistic expressions with these elements, is far less straightforward. The great number of proposed approaches already makes it clear that it is difficult to provide easily applicable and generally accepted annotation guidelines, which can easily be implemented in a web-based environment. An ideal discourse annotation system would be straightforward to use, and it would not require any learning – in the same way that using hyperlinks is a straightforward way to create references. Such an annotation model should also provide a substantial improvement to users who want to find relevant new knowledge.

Here, we propose a simple discourse annotation model to detect the main new knowledge claims in biology research papers. We also propose some suggestions for the implementation of the automatic detection of this model.

2 Claimed Knowledge Updates

Biomedical articles contain a great number of biological propositions, but not all of them are equally relevant: some are central claims, while others merely support the findings; some are factual, while others are merely hypothesized. The authors often summarize their main findings in the title, section titles and caption titles. In addition to these – structurally defined – summaries, the authors also formulate their main findings in rhetorically salient sentences. This rhetorical salience is conveyed via metadiscourse, by which the authors explicitly attribute the findings to themselves, and state that they are based on the current empirical work, such as: "*Our results demonstrate*", "*In the present study we identified*". We will call biological propositions summarized in such structurally or rhetorically salient sentences Claimed Knowledge Updates (CKU).

We hypothesize that a listing of the CKUs in a paper constitutes new main knowledge provided in that paper, and thus we propose that their detection may play an important role in text mining.

We define CKUs as follows:

1. A CKU expresses a verbal or nominal proposition about biological entities.
2. A CKU is a new proposition.
3. The authors present the CKU as factual.
4. A CKU is derived from the experimental work described in the article.
5. The ownership of the proposition is attributed to the author(s) of the article.
6. 4) and 5) are either explicitly expressed or are implicitly conveyed by a structural position as title, section or caption title.

Sentence	CKU
Here we used mass spectrometry to **identify**HuD as a novel neuronal SMN-interacting partner.	HuD is a neuronal SMN-interacting partner.
Our analysis of known HuD-associated mRNAs in neurons **identified** cpg15 mRNA as a highly abundant mRNA in HuDIPs compared with other known targets of HuD, such as GAP43 and Tau.	cpg15 mRNA is a highly abundant mRNA in HuDIPs
Our finding that SMN protein associates with HuD protein and the HuD target cpg15 mRNA in neurons led us to ask whether SMN deficiency affects the abundance or cellular distribution of cpg15 mRNA.	SMN protein associates with HuD protein
	SMN protein associates with cpg15 mRNA

Table 1. Sentences and CKUs from Akten et al.

As an example, Table 1 contains some CKUs from an article on Spinal Muscular Atrophy (Akten et al., 2011). The metadiscourse indicating CKUs is given in bold.

In studying this paper, we found a striking regularity in the appearance of CKUs throughout the article: the Abstract, the Introduction, the Results and the Discussion sections are repeat the same CKUs, as follows:

- in the Abstract they appear as a list of findings;
- in the Introduction, they are inserted within the context of previous knowledge;
- in the Results section, they are explained within the context of the authors' work, and thus provide empirical evidence;

and finally,

- in the Discussion, they are presented in the perspective of the advances in the research domain.

In other words, the four predefined structural units of research articles give an indicator of the underlying CKU organization. This regularity shows that rhetorical salience is systematically related to structural organization, and thus that the placement of the CKUs in the text can be a marker for discourse structure in biological research articles.

3 Automatic detection of CKUs

According to our definition, a CKU is a factual proposition referring to a bio-event, and its discourse function is updating knowledge: its source is the author of the current article, and its basis is the experimental findings of the current

Title	Abstract	Introduction	Results	Figures	Discussion	Citation	Event representation
Interaction of survival of motor neuron (SMN) and HuD proteins [with m RNA cpg15rescue s motor neuron axonal deficits]	Here **we** used mass spectrometry to **identify***HuD as* a novel *neuronal SMN-interacting partner.*	Here **we identify***HuD asa* novel *interacting partner of SMN,*	Together with our co-IP data, **these results indicate** that *SMN associates with HuD in motor neurons*	*SMN interacts with HuD.*	**Our** MS and co-IP **data demonstrat e** a strong **interaction between SMN and HuD** in spinal motor neuron axons.	Furthermore, **these findings** are consistent with recent studies **demonstrati ng** that *the interaction of HuD with the spinal muscular atrophy (SMA) protein SMN* ...	Entity1: HuD Entity2: SMN Relation: Interaction Location: Motor neurons

Table 2. The same bio-event repeated in the different sections of the paper, a citation, and its representation

article, and its basis is the experimental findings of the current article. The discourse function is indicated either by the proposition's structural position within the article or by metadiscourse.

We suggest detecting CKUs in three steps, combining state-of-the art document processing tools:

1. identifying structural discourse markers;
2. identifying rhetorical discourse markers,
3. extracting factual bio-events.

Structural indicators, i.e. the title, section titles or figure captions, are detected through markup in a straightforward way, if the article is encoded in a structured document format (e.g., XML). If this is not the case, a special conversion tool should be applied, as described in e.g. Déjean and Meunier (2007) to convert unstructured documents to structured documents.

Metadiscourse indicators, which convey both that the source of the new knowledge is attributed to the author(s) and that it is factual, such as "*here we demonstrate*", "*our results identify*", etc. could be detected by local pattern-matching rules in the majority of cases, since the authors often use highly recurring forms to express them. However, in some cases the expressions are somewhat more complex, and thus do not match local patterns. In order to ensure better performance, which is important due to the relevance and relatively small number of the claims to detect, we could apply the concept-matching methodology as described in Sándor (2007), which takes syntactic dependencies into account. This methodology consists of identifying specific kinds of metadiscourse as the realizations of patterns of concepts, which are present as semantic features in syntactically connected words and expressions.

To detect CKUs, we assume that these are indicated minimally by two co-occurring concepts: a first concept, which we call DEICTIC, and which conveys reference to the current work (*here, we, our, these*), and a second concept, which is a subclass of what we call MENTAL_OPERATION (*identify, demonstrate, find*, etc.). This specific subclass is a list of verbs and their nominalizations that belong to the category of "certainty verbs" in Thomas and Hawes (1994). This minimal pattern detects expressions like "*we identify*" or "*our finding*". In expressions like "*these results indicate*" or "*our data demonstrate*", the DEICTIC concept is linked to the certainty verb in an indirect way, since it is the modifier of the subject of the certainty verb.

This subject refers to the "base" factor of the bio-event (i.e. the indication comes from "results", and the demonstration from "data", see De Waard and Pander Maat (2009)), and thus it is also part of the metadiscourse. Its relevant semantic feature is called SCOPE in the concept-matching systems. In summary, CKU-specific metadiscourse is covered by the pattern DEICTIC + SCOPE + MENTAL_OPERATION, where the "+" sign indicates a syntactic relationship.

Consider the three sentences containing CKUs in Table 1. The metadiscourse is in bold:

(1) **Here we** used mass spectrometry to **identify** HuD as a novel neuronal SMN-interacting partner.

(2) **Our analysis** of known HuD-associated mRNAs in neurons **identified** cpg15 mRNA as a highly abundant mRNA in HuDIPs compared with other known targets of HuD, such as GAP43 and Tau.

(3) Together with our co-IP data, **these results indicate** that SMN associates with HuDin motor neurons, and that these two proteins colocalize in granules within motor neuron axons.

While (3) follows a straightforward local pattern, in sentences (1) and (2) the relationship between "we" and "identify" and "our analysis" and "identify" needs deep syntactic analysis. This analysis is carried out by the Xerox Incremental Parser (XIP) (Aït et al. 2000), on top of which we have implemented concept-matching rules for detecting metadiscourse indicating CKUs.

We developed a simple concept-matching grammar based on the rules described above, and assessed the results of the automatic detection of the rhetorical indicators of CKUs in two papers. With respect to our manual annotation of CKUs the coverage is 81% and 80% and the precision is 62% and 51% respectively.

Once the metadiscourse is detected, another module should be applied for detecting bio-events, i.e. factual propositions that involve biological entities. This step can be executed by a state-of-the-art biological parser that detects factual bio-events, like the one by Nawaz et al. (2010). Subsequent integration of factual bio-event extraction should improve the precision, because the metadiscourse by itself does not guarantee the factuality of the bio-events, as in the following sentence:

(4) **Our findings provide** further support for the hypothesis that SMN can associate with multiple RBPs to regulate axonal mRNA levels in neurons, and that the different SMN–RBP complexes may be defined by their mRNA contents.

4 Validation: are CKUs indeed the main claims?

To test whether CKUs represent indeed the main claims of biology papers we carried out the following checks:

1. First, we asked a domain specialist both to validate the CKUs as main claims, and select them in two of full-text papers.
2. Second, we analyzed how a source paper is cited in other papers, and investigated whether the descriptions given in the referring texts correspond to the CKUs in the cited papers.

We discuss these forms of validation in turn.

4.1 Validation by domain specialists

We carried out the validation in two steps. In the first step we manually highlighted the CKUs in two papers according to the definition given in section 2, above, and asked a biologist to select the sentences that were relevant claims of the article. In this step all the CKUs have been validated. This indicates that if biologists are provided with a list of CKUs annotated by non-specialists based on discourse indicators, they do get access to relevant claims of the articles.

In the second step we asked the biologist to highlight the sentences that conform to the 6 points of our definition of CKUs. In the first article she selected 26 sentences, out of which only 12 sentences were conform to the definition of CKUs. The article contains 4 further CKUs, which the biologist did not select. Out of the 14 sentences that were highlighted by the biologist and that did not satisfy the definition of CKUs, 5 do not satisfy one important criterion of CKUs, that of factuality. The remaining 9 sentences were factual, but did not explicitly attribute the proposition to the authors of the article, i.e. did not contain metadiscourse that characterizes CKUs. In the second article the biologist selected 48 sentences, out of which 24 were indeed CKUs, and there is no more CKU is the article. Similarly to the first article, 3 out of the remaining sentences were not factual and 21 did not contain metadiscourse.

This experiment leads us to three interesting observations:

1. A list of CKUs is meaningful for the biologist, however, CKUs do not provide an exhaustive and well-definable list of main claims.

2. The definition of the CKUs is difficult to apply for a biologist who is not trained in rhetorical analysis.
3. The notion of a "main claim" is not straightforward to define formally.

4.2 Citing sentences collection

Work on citation-based summarization (e.g. Kaplan et al., 2009, Jbara and Radev, 2011, Nakov et al., 2004) focuses on creating 'a summation of multiple scholars' viewpoints [...] using its set of citation sentences'. If we accept the premise of this work, which is that a collection of citation sentences offer a good overview of the cited papers, then CKUs should be well-represented in the collection of cited sentences. As a second check, we identified a collection of 20 citations of a full-text paper (Voorhoeve et al., 2006) and compared the citing sentences to the CKUs detected in this paper. We found that in all cases the citing sentences could be linked back to the CKUs (and indeed offer a good summary of the cited paper).

5 Discussion

5.1 Related work

De Waard and Pander Maat (2012) propose a model for epistemic classification of bio-events that consists of three parts: epistemic value (from factual through various degrees of certainty until lack of knowledge); base (grounding for the knowledge: reasoning, data or unidentified); source (author, named external source, implicit, attribution to the author, nameless external source, no source of knowledge). Each bio-event is characterized by a combination of the three factors. CKUs represent a special case in this system: their epistemic value is factual, their base is data derived from the work described in the article, and their source is the author. Whereas De Waard and Pander Maat do not differentiate among the various combinations of the factors, we propose to handle this unique combination on its own right, since it fulfills a special discourse function in the article, which facilitates access to the main claims.

Each of the three factors that characterize CKUs is taken into account in various text-mining systems, however, to our knowledge, no other system defines a discourse function in terms of these three factors. Nawaz et al. (2010) detect factual bio-events, but they do not detect authorship and base. The same holds for the annotation guidelines developed by and Wilbur et al. (2006). Teufel (2000) considers authorship but does not consider factuality and base. Blake (2010) differentiates among several kinds of base and considers only factual bio-events, but does not consider authorship.

Jaime-Sisó (2011) makes the same observation as we do: the authors summarize and repeat the main findings in every section of the articles. She attributes this phenomenon to the authors' adaptation to electronic publishing, where there is the possibility to navigate in the text. Repetition facilitates this navigation. Based on interviews with researchers and the analysis of 20 biology articles, she concludes that summarizing sentences that repeat the main findings in each section of biology articles are crucial both in writing and reading practices: "Aware of the scientists' reading practices, both editors and writers contribute to ensure that, whatever section of the text is scanned, and regardless of the reasons of approaching the article, the reader obtains the most newsworthy information, as if each of the sections could stand alone." (p. 87) "Noteworthy information" is mostly expressed by CKUs, although Jaime-Sisó does not provide a rhetorically based definition of summarizing sentences.

5.2 Proposed applications

We argue that the detection of Claimed Knowledge Updates constitutes a relevant goal for text-mining. CKUs are systematically signaled either by their position within the paper or by specific rhetorical discourse markers. This demonstrates that they constitute a systematic discourse organizing factor of articles. Moreover, CKUs can be detected by integrating state-of-the-art tools.

The detection of new factual knowledge could be useful in several tasks, such as summarization, information extraction, updating ontologies and knowledge bases, etc.

In particular, we wish to propose two use cases: first, the identification of CKUs could improve the output of automated knowledge bases that rely on text mining. Several text mining systems aim to provide multi-dimensional characterizations of bio-events, both academic systems such as

MEDIE[1]and iHoP[2], and commercial systems such as Ariadne[3]and BEL[4]. In none of these systems, however, are the various bio-events detected differentiated according to their role in updating knowledge. Showing only the CKUs, and not all the claims, would greatly enhance the efficiency and use of these automated knowledge bases. For example, the output of the query 'LATS2' as a subject in MEDIE returned the following sentences:

1. LATS2 is a member of the LATS tumor suppressor family.
2. The differences in the expression levels of the LATS2, S100A2 and hTERT genes in different types of NSCLC are significant.
3. LATS2 is a new member of the LATS tumour suppressor family.
4. Among the growing list of putative Mdm2-regulated proteins are several proteins playing a key role in the control of cell proliferation such as pRb, E2F1/DP1, Numb, Smads, Lats2 or IGF-1R.
5. In addition, modulation of novel target genes such as LATS2 and GREB1 were identified to be mediated by Nrf2.
6. Here, we show that LATS proteins (mammalian orthologs of Warts) interact directly with YAP in mammalian cells and that ectopic expression of LATS1, but not LATS2, effectively suppresses the YAP phenotypes
7. The tumor suppressor genes NEO1 and LATS2, and the estrogen receptor gene ESR1, all have binding sites for p53 and hsa-mir-372/373.

It is clear - even without studying the textual context - that not all of these sentences refer to a new finding pertaining to LATS2, which is what the user would like to see, and what a CKU parser would provide.

A second possible application of CKU detection could be the presentation of CKUs as metadata in biomedical publications, to aid the navigation within and among collections of biology articles. This is illustrated in a mock-up (Figure), which extends the PNAS publication scheme with an additional column presenting CKUs. The column in the middle is a part of the standard PNAS layout, and it points to the past, i.e. to existing articles that the current article draws on. But the third new column on the right extracts CKUs put forward in the current article. According to where the CKUs are, the readers can learn what type of arguments they could find to support them in the text to the left: in the introduction - background knowledge; in the results - experiments; in the discussion - various other links and implications; in the Figures - the illustration of the experiments.

To support both of these applications, CKUs could be marked up by the authors of the article during authoring or submission, making use of tools that identify CKUs. The systematic annotation of CKUs by the authors could provide them with a structural template against which they could check the article's coherence, and act in a role similar to a Structured Digital Abstract, proposed by Gerstein et al. (2007), as a 'computer-readable summary of pertinent facts'. These CKUs could then be added directly to a bio-event representation framework, where biological entities, interaction types, locations, etc. are structurally marked for easy information extraction. In this way, the user can easily track the grounding of a specific bio-event in past work, present experiments and future possibilities– and eventually, do better science.

---

[1]http://www.nactem.ac.uk/medie/
[2]http://www.ihop-net.org/UniPub/iHOP/
[3]http://www.ariadnegenomics.com/
[4] http://www.openbel.org

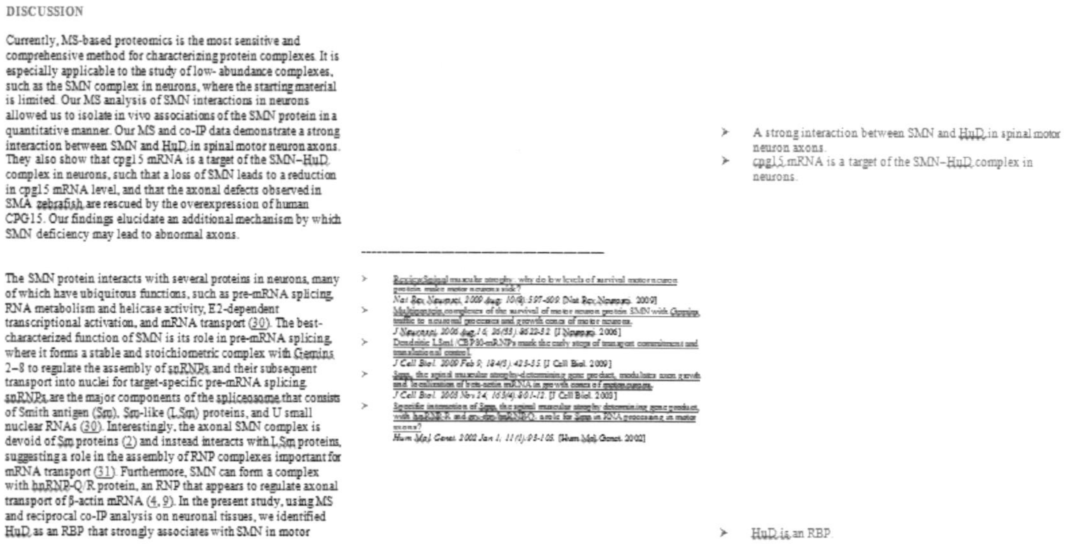

Figure Mockup of presenting CKUs in publications

Acknowledgements

We are indebted and deeply grateful to Prof. Maryanne Martone from the University of San Diego for her generous help in annotating the CKUs in our texts, and to our anonymous reviewers for helping us improve this paper.

References

Salah Aït-Mokhtar, Jean-Pierre Chanod, and Claude Roux. 2002. Robustness beyond shallowness: incremental dependency parsing. Natural Language Engineering, 8(2/3):121-144.

Amjad Abu-Jbara and Dragomir Radev. 2011. Coherent Citation-Based Summarization of Scientific Papers. Proceedings of the 49th Annual Meeting of the Association for Computational Linguistics, pages 500–509, Portland, Oregon, June 19-24, 2011

Akten, Bikem, Min JeongKye, Le T. Hao, Mary H. Wertz, Sasha Singh, DuyuNie, Jia Huang, Tanuja T. Merianda, Jeffery L. Twiss, Christine E. Beattie, Judith A. J. Steen, and Mustafa Sahin. 2011. Interaction of survival of motor neuron (SMN) and HuD proteins with mRNA cpg15 rescues motor neuron axonal deficits, ProcNatlAcadSci U S A. 2011 Jun 21;108(25):10337-42.

Catherine Blake. 2010. Beyond genes, proteins, and abstracts: Identifying scientific claims from full-text biomedical articles. Journal of Biomedical Informatics archive Volume 43 Issue 2, April, 2010

Pablo Ciccarese, Elizabeth Wu, June Kinoshita, Gwen Wong, Marco Ocana, Alan Ruttenberg, and Tim Clark. 2008. The SWAN Biomedical Discourse Ontology.J Biomed Inform. 2008 Oct;41(5):739-51. Epub 2008 May 4.. PMID: 18583197

HervéDejean and Jean-Luc Meunier. 2007. Logical Document conversion: combining functional and formal knowledge. Symposium on Document Engineering, Winnipeg, Canada, August 28-31, 2007.

Mark Gerstein, Michael Seringhausand and Stanley Field. 2007. Structured digital abstract makes text mining easy, *Nature* 447, 142 (10 May 2007) | doi:10.1038/447142a

Mercedes Jaime-Sisó. 2011. Summarizing Findings: An All-Pervasive Move In Open Access Biomedical Research Articles Involves Rephrasing Strategies. In Researching Specialized Languages.Studies in Corpus Linguistics 47.Edited by Bhatia, Vijay, Sánchez Hernández, Purificación and Pérez-Paredes, Pascual.Published by John Benjamins. Pp. 71-88.

Amjadabu Jbara and Dragomir R. Radev. 2011. Coherent citation-based summarization of scientific papers. In Proceedings of ACL 2011, Portland, Oregon, 2011.

Dain Kaplan, Ryu Iida and Takenobu Tokunaga. 2009. Automatic Extraction of Citation Contexts for Research Paper Summarization: A Coreference-chain based Approach, Proceedings of the 2009 Workshop on Text and Citation Analysis for Scholarly Digital Libraries, ACL-IJCNLP 2009, pages 88–95, Suntec, Singapore, 7 August 2009.

Maria Liakata, Simone Teufel, Advaith Siddharthan and Colin Batchelor. 2010. Corpora for conceptualisation and zoning of scientific papersProceedings of the Seventh conference on International Language Resources and Evaluation (LREC'10), Malta.

Yoko Mizuta, Anna Korhonen, Tony Mullen, and Nigel Collier. 2006. Zone analysis in biology articles as a basis for information extraction.International Journal of Medical Informatics. 75(6): 468-487.

Preslav I. Nakov, Ariel S. Schwartz, A., and Marti Hearst. 2004. Citances: Citation Sentences for Semantic Analysis of Bioscience Text, in the SIGIR'04 Workshop on Search and Discovery in Bioinformatics.

Raheel Nawaz, Paul Thompson, John McNaught, Sophia Ananiadou. 2010. Meta-Knowledge Annotation of Bio-Events. Proceedings of the Seventh International Conference on Language Resources and Evaluation (LREC 2010).

Cameron Neylon. 2012. Network Enabled Research: Maximise scale and connectivity, minimise friction, Blog post, February 2012, http://cameronneylon.net/blog/network-enabled-research/

Ágnes Sándor. 2007. Modeling metadiscourse conveying the author's rhetorical strategy in biomedical research abstracts. Revue Française de Linguistique Appliquée 200(2):97--109.

Simone Teufel. 1999. Argumentative Zoning: Information Extraction from ScientificText. PhD Thesis.

Simone Teufel and Marc Moens. 2000. What's yours and what's mine: Determining intellectual attribution in scientific text. Proceedings of the 2000 Joint SIGDAT conference on Empirical methods in natural language processing and very large corpora.

Sarah Thomas and Thomas P. Hawes. 1994. Reporting Verbs in Medical Journal Articles. English for Specific Purposes, v13 n2 p129-48 1994.

P. Mathijs Voorhoeve, Carlos le Sage, et. Al. 2006. A genetic screen implicates miRNA-372 and miRNA-373 as oncogenes in testicular germ cell tumors. *Cell.* 2006 Mar 24;124(6):1169-81.

Anita de Waard, Simon Buckingham Shum, Annamaria Carusi, Jack Park, Mathias Samwald, and Ágnes Sándor. 2009. Hypotheses, evidence and relationships: The HypER approach for representing scientific knowledge claims. In: Proceedings 8th International Semantic Web Conference, Workshop on Semantic Web Applications in Scientific Discourse. Lecture Notes in Computer Science, Springer Verlag: Berlin, 26 Oct 2009, Washington DC.

Anita de Waard and Henk Pander Maat 2009. Categorizing Epistemic Segment Types in Biology Research Articles. Workshop on Linguistic and Psycholinguistic Approaches to Text Structuring (LPTS 2009), September 21-23 2009

Anita de Waard,. and Pander Maat., H.P.M., 2012. Workshop on Detecting Structure in Scientific Discourse, ACL 2012, Jeju Island, Korea (this workshop).

W. John Wilbur, Andrey Rzhetsky and Hagit Shatkay. 2006. New directions in biomedical text annotation: definitions, guidelines and corpus construction, BMC Bioinformatics, vol. 7, no. (356)

Detection of Implicit Citations for Sentiment Detection

Awais Athar **Simone Teufel**
Computer Laboratory, University of Cambridge
15 JJ Thomson Avenue, Cambridge CB3 0FD, UK
{awais.athar,simone.teufel}@cl.cam.ac.uk

Abstract

Sentiment analysis of citations in scientific papers is a new and interesting problem which can open up many exciting new applications in bibliometrics. Current research assumes that using just the citation sentence is enough for detecting sentiment. In this paper, we show that this approach misses much of the existing sentiment. We present a new corpus in which all mentions of a cited paper have been annotated. We explore methods to automatically identify these mentions and show that the inclusion of implicit citations in citation sentiment analysis improves the quality of the overall sentiment assignment.

1 Introduction

The idea of using citations as a source of information has been explored extensively in the field of bibliometrics, and more recently in the field of computational linguistics. State-of-the-art citations identification mechanisms focus either on detecting explicit citations i.e. those that consist of either the author names and the year of publication or bracketed numbers only, or include a small sentence window around the explicit citation as input text (Councill et al., 2008; Radev et al., 2009; Ritchie et al., 2008). The assumption behind this approach is that all related mentions of the paper would be concentrated in the immediate vicinity of the anchor text. However, this assumption does not generally hold true (Teufel, 2010; Sugiyama et al., 2010). The phenomenon of trying to determine a citations's *citation context* has a long tradition in library sciences (O'Connor, 1982), and its connection with coreference has been duely noted (Kim et al., 2006; Kaplan et al., 2009). Consider Figure 1, which illustrates a typical case.

> grams. In order to improve sentence-level evaluation performance, several metrics have been proposed, including ROUGE-W, ROUGE-S (Lin and Och, 2004) and METEOR (Banerjee and Lavie, 2005). ROUGE-W differs from BLEU and NIST
>
> ⋮
>
> METEOR is essentially a unigram based metric, which prefers the monotonic word alignment between MT output and the references by penalizing crossing word alignments. There are two problems with METEOR. First, it doesn't consider gaps in the aligned words, which is an important feature for evaluating the sentence fluency; second, it cannot use multiple references simultaneously.[1] ROUGE and METEOR both use WordNet

Figure 1: Example of the use of anaphora

While the first sentence cites the target paper explicitly using the name of the primary author along with the year of publication of the paper, the remaining sentences mentioning the same paper appear after a gap and contain an indirect and implicit reference to that paper. These mentions occur two sentences after the formal citation in the form of anaphoric *it* and the lexical hook *METEOR*. Most current techniques, with the exception of Qazvinian and Radev (2010), are not able to detect linguistic mentions of citations in such forms. Ignoring such mentions and examining only the sentences containing an explicit citation results in loss of information about the cited paper. While this phenomenon is problematic for applications like scientific summarisation (Abu-Jbara and Radev, 2011), it has a particular relevance for citation sentiment detection (Athar, 2011).

Citation sentiment detection is an attractive task. Availability of citation polarity information can help researchers in understanding the evolution of a field on the basis of research papers and their critiques. It can also help expert researchers who are in the process of preparing opinion based summaries for survey papers by providing them with motivations behind as well as positive and negative comments about different approaches (Qazvinian and Radev, 2008).

Current work on citation sentiment detection works under the assumption that the sentiment present in the citation sentence represents the true sentiment of the author towards the cited paper (Athar, 2011; Piao et al., 2007; Pham and Hoffmann, 2004). This assumption is so dominant because current citation identification methods (Councill et al., 2008; Ritchie et al., 2008; Radev et al., 2009) can readily identify the citation sentence, whereas it is much harder to determine the relevant context. However, this assumption most certainly does not hold true when the citation context spans more than one sentence.

Concerning the sentiment aspect of the citation context from Figure 1, we see that the citation sentence does not contain any sentiment towards the cited paper, whereas the following sentences act as a critique and list its shortcomings. It is clear that criticism is the intended sentiment, but if the gold standard is defined by looking at the citation sentence in isolation, a significant amount of sentiment expressed in the text is lost. Given that overall most citations in a text are neutral with respect to sentiment (Spiegel-Rosing, 1977; Teufel et al., 2006), this makes it even more important to recover what explicit sentiment there is in the article, wherever it is to be found.

In this paper, we examine methods to extract all opinionated sentences from research papers which mention a given paper in as many forms as we can identify, not just as explicit citations. We present a new corpus in which all mentions of a cited paper have been manually annotated, and show that our annotation treatment increases citation sentiment coverage, particularly for negative sentiment. We then explore methods to automatically identify all mentions of a paper in a supervised manner. In particular, we consider the recognition of named approaches and acronyms. Our overall system then classifies explicit and implicit mentions according to sentiment. The results support the claim that including implicit citations in citation sentiment analysis improves the quality of the overall sentiment assignment.

2 Corpus Construction

We use the dataset from Athar (2011) as our starting point, which consists of 8,736 citations in the ACL Anthology (Bird et al., 2008) that cite a target set of 310 ACL Anthology papers. The citation summary data from the ACL Anthology Network[1] (Radev et al., 2009) is used. This dataset is rather large, and since manual annotation of context for each citation is a time consuming task, a subset of 20 target papers (i.e., all citations to these) has been selected for annotation. These 20 papers correspond to approximately 20% of incoming citations in the original dataset. They contain a total of 1,555 citations from 854 citing papers.

2.1 Annotation

We use a four-class scheme for annotation. Every sentence which does not contain any direct or indirect mention of the citation is labelled as being excluded (x) from the context. The rest of the sentences are marked either positive (p), negative (n) or objective/neutral (o). To speed up the annotation process, we developed a customised annotation tool.

A total of 203,803 sentences have been annotated from 1,034 paper–reference pairs. Although this annotation been performed by the first author only, we know from previous work that similar styles of annotation can achieve acceptable inter-annotator agreement (Teufel et al., 2006). An example annotation is given in Figure 2, where the first column shows the line number and the second one shows the class label for the citation to *Smadja (1993)*. It should be noted that since annotation is always per-

[1] http://www.aclweb.org

formed for a specific citation only, sentences such as the one at line 32, which carry sentiment but refer to a different citation, are marked as excluded from the context.

If there are multiple sentiments in the same sentence, the sentence has been labelled with the class of the last sentiment mentioned. In this way, a total of 3,760 citation sentences have been found in the whole corpus, i.e. sentences belonging to class *o*, *n* or *p*, and the rest have been labelled as *x*. Table 1 compares the number of sentences with only the explicit citations with all explicit and implicit mentions of those citations. We can see that including the citation context increases the subjective sentiment by almost 185%. The resulting negative sentiment also increases by more than 325%. This may be attributed to the strategic behaviour of the authors of 'sweetening' the criticism in order to soften its effects among their peers (Hornsey et al., 2008).

31	*x*	Church and Hanks (Church and Hanks 1990) employed mutual information to extract both adjacent and distant bi-grams that tend to co-occur within a fixed-size window.
32	*x*	But the method did not extend to extract n-grams.
33	*o*	**Smadja (Smadja 1993) proposed a statistical model by measuring the spread of the distribution of cooccurring pairs of words with higher strength.**
34	*p*	This method successfully extracted both adjacent and distant bi-grams and n-grams.
35	*n*	However, the method failed to extract bi-grams with lower frequency.

Figure 2: Example annotation of a citation context.

	Explicit mentions	All mentions
o	$1,509$	$3,100$
n	86	368
p	146	292

Table 1: Distribution of classes.

Another view of the annotated data is available in Figure 3a. This is in the form of interactive HTML where each HTML page represents all the incoming links to a paper. Each row represents the citing paper and each column square represents a sentence. The rows are sorted by increasing publication date. Black squares are citations with the author name and year of publication mentioned in the text. The red, green and gray squares show negative, positive and neutral sentiment respectively. Pointing the mouse cursor at any square gives the text content of the corresponding sentence, as shown in the Figure 3a.

The ACL Id, paper title and authors' names are also given at the top of the page. Similar data for the corresponding citing paper is made available when the mouse cursor is positioned on one of the orange squares at the start of each row, as shown in the Figure 3b. Clicking on the checkboxes at the top hides or shows the corresponding type of squares. There is also an option to hide/show a grid so that the squares are separated and rows are easier to trace. For example, Figure 3b shows the grid with the neutral or objective citations hidden.

In the next section, we describe the features set we use to detect implicit citations from this annotated corpus and discuss the results.

3 Experiments and Results

For the task of detecting all mentions of a citation, we merge the class labels of sentences mentioning a citation in any form (o_n_p). To make sure that the easily detectable explicit citations do not influence the results, we change the class label of all those sentences to x which contain the first author's name within a 4-word window of the year of publication.

Our dataset is skewed as there are many more objective sentences than subjective ones. In such scenarios, average *micro-F* scores tend to be slightly higher as they are a weighted measure. To avoid this bias, we also report the *macro-F* scores. Furthermore, to ensure there is enough data for training each class, we use 10-fold cross-validation (Lewis, 1991) in all our experiments.

We represent each citation as a feature set in a Support Vector Machine (SVM) (Cortes and Vapnik, 1995) framework. The corpus is processed using WEKA (Hall et al., 2008) and the Weka LibSVM library (EL-Manzalawy and Honavar, 2005; Chang and Lin, 2001). For each ith sentence S_i, we use the following binary features.

- S_{i-1} *contains the last name of the primary author, followed by the year of publication within a four-word window.*

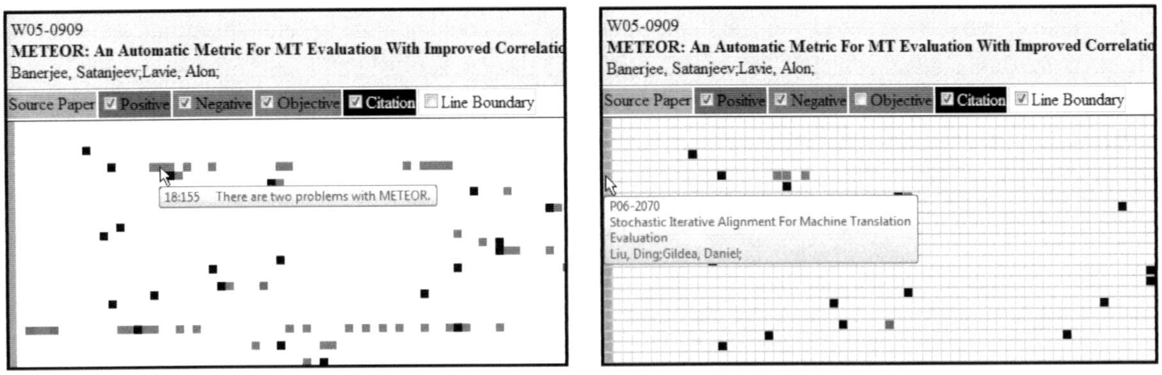

(a) Sentence Text

(b) Paper metadata

Figure 3: Different views of an annotated paper.

This feature is meant to capture the fact that the sentence immediately after an explicit citation is more likely to continue talking about the same work.

- *S_i contains the last name of the primary author followed by the year of publication within a four-word window.*

  This feature should help in identifying sentences containing explicit citations. Since such sentences are easier to identify, including them in the evaluation metric would result in a false boost in the final score. We have thus excluded all such sentences in our annotation and this feature should indicate a negative instance to the classifier.

- *S_i contains the last name of the primary author.*

  This feature captures sentences which contain a reference to tools and algorithms which have been named after their inventors, such as,

  "One possible direction for future work is to compare the search-based approach of ***Collins and Roark*** *with our DP-based approach."*

  It should also capture the mentions of methods and techniques used in the cited paper e.g.,

  "We show that our approach outperforms ***Turney****'s approach."*

- *S_i contains an acronym used in an explicit citation.*

  Acronyms are taken to be capitalised words which are extracted from the vicinity of the cited author's last name using regular expressions. For example, *METEOR* in Figure 1 is an acronym which is used in place of a formal citation to refer to the original paper in the rest of the citing paper.

- *S_i contains a determiner followed by a work noun.*

  We use the following determiners D = {*the, this, that, those, these, his, her, their, such, previous, other*}. The list of work nouns (*technique, method, etc.*) has been taken from Teufel (2010). This feature extracts a pattern which has been found to be useful for extracting citations in previous work (Qazvinian and Radev, 2010). Such phrases usually signal a continuation of the topics related to citations in earlier sentences. For example:

  "Church et al.(1989), Wettler & Rapp (1989) and Church & Hanks (1990) describe algorithms which do this. However, the validity of ***these algorithms*** *has not been tested by systematic comparisons with associations of human subjects."*

- *S_i starts with a third person pronoun.*

  The feature also tries to capture the topic continuation after a citation. Sentences starting with a pronoun (e.g. *they, their, he, she, etc.*) are more likely to describe the subject citation of the previous sentence in detail. For example:

*"Because Daume III (2007) views the adaptation as merely augmenting the feature space, each of his features has the same prior mean and variance, regardless of whether it is domain specific or independent. **He** could have set these parameters differently, but he did not."*

- *S_i starts with a connector.*

  This feature also focuses on detecting the topic continuity. Connectors have been shown to be effective in other context related works as well (Hatzivassiloglou and McKeown, 1997; Polanyi and Zaenen, 2006). A list of 23 connectors (e.g. *however, although, moreover, etc.*) has been compiled by examining the high frequency connectors from a separate set of papers from the same domain. An example is:

  *"An additional consistent edge of a linear-chain conditional random field (CRF) explicitly models the dependencies between distant occurrences of similar words (Sutton and McCallum, 2004; Finkel et al. , 2005). **However**, this approach requires additional time complexity in inference/learning time and it is only suitable for representing constraints by enforcing label consistency."*

- *S_i starts with a (sub)section heading.*

- *S_{i-1} starts with a (sub)section heading.*

- *S_{i+1} starts with a (sub)section heading.*

  The three features above are a consequence of missing information about the paragraph and section boundaries in the used corpus. Since the text extraction has been done automatically, the section headings are usually found to be merged with the text of the succeeding sentence. For example, the text below merges the heading of section 4.2 with the next sentence.

  "4.2 METEOR vs. SIA SIA is designed to take the advantage of loose sequence-based metrics without losing word-level information."

  Start and end of such section boundaries can give us important information about the scope of a citation. In order to exploit this information, we use regular expressions to detect if the sentences under review contains these merged section titles and headings.

- *S_i contains a citation other than the one under review.*

  It is more probable for the context of a citation to end when other citations are mentioned in a sentence, which is the motivation behind using this feature, which might contribute to the discriminating power of the classifier in conjunction with the presence of a citation in the previous sentence. For example, in the extract below, the scope of the first citation is limited to the first sentence only.

  *"Blitzer et al.(2006) proposed a structural correspondence learning method for domain adaptation and applied it to part-of-speech tagging. **Daume III (2007)** proposed a simple feature augmentation method to achieve domain adaptation."*

- *S_i contains a lexical hook.*

  The lexical hooks feature identifies lexical substitutes for the citations. We obtain these hooks by examining all explicit citation sentences to the cited paper and selecting the most frequent capitalized phrase in the vicinity of the author's last name. The explicit citations come from all citing papers and not just the paper for which the features are being determined. For example, the sentences below have been taken from two different papers and cite the same target paper (Cutting et al., 1992). While the acronym *HMM* will be captured by the feature stated earlier, the word *Xerox* will be missed.

  E95-1014: *"This text was part-of-speech tagged using the **Xerox** HMM tagger (Cutting et al. , 1992)."*
  J97-3003: *"The **Xerox** tagger (Cutting et al. 1992) comes with a set of rules that assign an unknown word a set of possible pos-tags (i.e. , POS-class) on the basis of its ending segment."*

  This 'domain level' feature makes it possible to extract the commonly used name for a technique which may have been missed by the acronym feature due to long term dependencies. We also extrapolate the acronym for such phrases, e.g., in the example below, *SCL* would also be checked along with *Structural Correspondence Learning*.

"The paper compares ***Structural Correspondence Learning*** *(Blitzer et al., 2006) with (various instances of) self-training (Abney, 2007; McClosky et al., 2006) for the adaptation of a parse selection model to Wikipedia domains"*

We also add n-grams of length 1 to 3 to this lexical feature set and compare the results obtained with an n-gram only baseline in Table 2. N-grams have been shown to perform consistently well in various NLP tasks (Bergsma et al., 2010).

Class	Baseline	Our System
x	0.995	0.996
o_n_p	0.358	0.513
$Avg.$	0.990	0.992
$Avg.(macro)$	0.677	0.754

Table 2: Comparison of F-scores for non-explicit citation detection.

By adding the new features listed above, the performance of our system increases by almost 8% over the n-gram baseline for the task of detecting citation mentions. Using the pairwise Wilcoxon rank-sum test at 0.05 significance level, we found that the difference between the baseline and our system is statistically significant[2]. While the *micro-F* score obtained is quite high, the individual class scores show that the task is hard and a better solution may require a deeper analysis of the context.

4 Impact on Citation Sentiment Detection

We explore the effect of this context on citation sentiment detection. For a baseline, we use features of the state-of-the-art system proposed in our earlier work (Athar, 2011). While there we used n-gram and dependency feature on sentences containing explicit citations only, our annotation is not restricted to such citations and we may have more than one sentiment per each explicit citation. For example, in Figure 2, our 2011 system will be restricted to analysing sentence 33 only. However, it is clear from our annotation that there is more sentiment present in the succeeding sentences which belongs to this explicit citation. While sentence 34 in Figure 2 is positive towards the cited paper, the next sentence criticises it. Thus for this explicit citation, there are three sentences with sentiment and all of them are related to the same explicit citation. Treating these sentences separately will result in an artificial increase in the amount of data because they participate in the same discourse. It would also make it impossible to compare the sentiment annotated in the previous work with our annotation.

To make sure the annotations are comparable, we mark the true citation sentiment to be the last sentiment mentioned in a 4-sentence context window, as this is pragmatically most likely to be the real intention (MacRoberts and MacRoberts, 1984). The window length is motivated by recent research (Qazvinian and Radev, 2010) which favours a four-sentence boundary for detecting non-explicit citations. Analysis of our data shows that more than 60% of the subjective citations lie in this window. We include the implicit citations predicted by the method described in the previous section in the context. The results of the single-sentence baseline system are compared with this context enhanced system in Table 3.

Class	Baseline	Our System
o	0.861	0.887
n	0.138	0.621
p	0.396	0.554
$Avg.$	0.689	0.807
$Avg.(macro)$	0.465	0.687

Table 3: F-scores for citation sentiment detection.

The results show that our system outperforms the baseline in all evaluation criteria. Performing the pairwise Wilcoxon rank-sum testat 0.05 significance level, we found that the improvement is statistically significant. The baseline system does not use any context and thus misses out on all the sentiment information contained within. While this window-based representation does not capture all the senti-

[2]While this test may not be adequate as the data is highly skewed, we are reporting the results since there is no obvious alternative for discrete skewed data. In future, we plan to use the continuous probability estimates produced by the classifier for testing significance.

ment towards a citation perfectly, it is closer to the truth than a system based on single sentence analysis and is able to detect more sentiment.

5 Related Work

While different schemes have been proposed for annotating citations according to their function (Spiegel-Rosing, 1977; Nanba and Okumura, 1999; Garzone and Mercer, 2000), the only recent work on citation sentiment detection using a relatively large corpus is by Athar (2011). However, this work does not handle citation context. Other approaches to citation classification include work by Wilbur et al. (2006), who annotated a 101 sentence corpus on focus, polarity, certainty, evidence and directionality. Piao et al. (2007) proposed a system to attach sentiment information to the citation links between biomedical papers by using existing semantic lexical resources and NLP tools.

A common approach for sentiment detection is to use a labelled lexicon to score sentences (Hatzivassiloglou and McKeown, 1997; Turney, 2002; Yu and Hatzivassiloglou, 2003). However, such approaches have been found to be highly topic dependent (Engström, 2004; Gamon and Aue, 2005; Blitzer et al., 2007), which makes the creation of a general sentiment classifier a difficult task.

Teufel et al. (2006) worked on a 2,829 sentence citation corpus using a 12-class classification scheme. While the authors did make use of the context in their annotation, their focus was on the task of determining the author's reason for citing a given paper. This task differs from citation sentiment detection, which is in a sense a "lower level" of analysis.

Some other recent work has focused on the problem of implicit citation extraction (Kaplan et al., 2009; Qazvinian and Radev, 2010). Kaplan et al. (2009) explore co-reference chains for citation extraction using a combination of co-reference resolution techniques (Soon et al., 2001; Ng and Cardie, 2002). However, the corpus that they use consists of only 94 citations to 4 papers and is likely to be too small to be representative.

For citation extraction, the most relevant work is by Qazvinian and Radev (2010) who proposed a framework of Markov Random Fields to extract only the non-explicit citations for a given paper. They model each sentence as a node in a graph and experiment with various window boundaries to create edges between neighbouring nodes weighted by lexical similarity between nodes. However, their dataset consists of only 569 citations from 10 papers and their annotation scheme deals with neither acronyms nor sentiment.

6 Discussion

What is the role of citation contexts in the overall structure of scientific context? We assume a hierarchical, rhetorical structure not unlike RST (Mann and Thompson, 1987), but much flatter, where the atomic units are textual blocks which carry a certain functional role in the overall scientific argument for publication (Teufel, 2010; Hyland, 2000). Under such a general model, citation blocks are certainly a functional unit, and their recognition is a rewarding task in their own right. If citation blocks can be recognised along with their sentiment, this is even more useful, as it restricts the possibilities for which rhetorical function the segment plays. For instance, in the motivation section of a paper, before the paper contribution is introduced, we often find negative sentiment assigned to citations, as any indication can serve as a justification for the current paper. In contrast, positive sentiment is more likely to be restricted to the description of an approach which the authors include in their solution, or further develop.

Another aspect concerns which features might help in detecting coherent citation blocks. We have here addressed coherence of citation contexts via certain referring expressions, lexical hooks and also coherence-indicating conjunctions (amongst others). The reintroduction of citation contexts was addressed via lexical hooks. Much more could be done to explore this very interesting question. A more fine-grained model of coherence might include proper anaphora resolution (Lee et al., 2011), which is still an unsolved task for scientific texts, and also include models of lexical coherence such as lexical chains (Barzilay and Elhadad, 1997) and entity coherence (Barzilay and Lapata, 2008).

7 Conclusion

In this paper, we focus on automatic detection of citation sentiment using citation context. We annotate a new large corpus and show that ignoring the citation context would result in loss of a lot of sentiment, specially criticism. We also report the results of the state-of-the-art citation sentiment detection systems on this corpus and when using this context-enhanced gold standard definition.

References

A. Abu-Jbara and D. Radev. 2011. Coherent citation-based summarization of scientific papers. In *Proc. of ACL*.

A. Athar. 2011. Sentiment analysis of citations using sentence structure-based features. In *Proc of ACL*, page 81.

Regina Barzilay and Michael Elhadad. 1997. Using lexical chains for text summarization. In Inderjeet Mani and Mark T. Maybury, editors, *Proceedings of the ACL/EACL-97 Workshop on Intelligent Scalable Text Summarization*.

Regina Barzilay and Mirella Lapata. 2008. Modeling local coherence: An entity-based approach. *Computational Linguistics*, (1):1–34.

Shane Bergsma, Emily Pitler, and Dekang Lin. 2010. Creating robust supervised classifiers via web-scale n-gram data. In *Proceedings of the 48th Annual Meeting of the Association for Computational Linguistics*, pages 865–874, Uppsala, Sweden, July. Association for Computational Linguistics.

S. Bird, R. Dale, B.J. Dorr, B. Gibson, M.T. Joseph, M.Y. Kan, D. Lee, B. Powley, D.R. Radev, and Y.F. Tan. 2008. The acl anthology reference corpus: A reference dataset for bibliographic research in computational linguistics. In *Proc. of LREC*.

J. Blitzer, M. Dredze, and F. Pereira. 2007. Biographies, bollywood, boom-boxes and blenders: Domain adaptation for sentiment classification. In *Proc. of ACL*, number 1.

C.C. Chang and C.J. Lin. 2001. LIBSVM: a library for support vector machines, 2001. *Software available at* `http://www.csie.ntu.edu.tw/cjlin/libsvm`.

C. Cortes and V. Vapnik. 1995. Support-vector networks. *Machine learning*, 20(3):273–297.

I.G. Councill, C.L. Giles, and M.Y. Kan. 2008. Parscit: An open-source crf reference string parsing package. In *Proc. of LREC*, volume 2008. Citeseer.

Y. EL-Manzalawy and V. Honavar, 2005. *WLSVM: Integrating LibSVM into Weka Environment*. Software available at `http://www.cs.iastate.edu/~yasser/wlsvm`.

C. Engström. 2004. Topic dependence in sentiment classification. *Unpublished MPhil Dissertation. University of Cambridge*.

M. Gamon and A. Aue. 2005. Automatic identification of sentiment vocabulary: exploiting low association with known sentiment terms. In *Proc. of the ACL*, pages 57–64.

M. Garzone and R. Mercer. 2000. Towards an automated citation classifier. *Advances in Artificial Intelligence*.

D. Hall, D. Jurafsky, and C.D. Manning. 2008. Studying the history of ideas using topic models. In *EMNLP*, pages 363–371.

V. Hatzivassiloglou and K.R. McKeown. 1997. Predicting the semantic orientation of adjectives. In *Proc. of ACL*, page 181.

M.J. Hornsey, E. Robson, J. Smith, S. Esposo, and R.M. Sutton. 2008. Sugaring the pill: Assessing rhetorical strategies designed to minimize defensive reactions to group criticism. *Human Communication Research*, 34(1):70–98.

Ken Hyland. 2000. *Disciplinary Discourses; Social Interaction in Academic Writing*. Longman, Harlow.

D. Kaplan, R. Iida, and T. Tokunaga. 2009. Automatic extraction of citation contexts for research paper summarization: A coreference-chain based approach. In *Proc. of the 2009 Workshop on Text and Citation Analysis for Scholarly Digital Libraries*.

D. Kim, P. Webber, et al. 2006. Implicit references to citations: A study of astronomy papers.

H. Lee, Y. Peirsman, A. Chang, N. Chambers, M. Surdeanu, and D. Jurafsky. 2011. Stanford's multi-pass sieve coreference resolution system at the conll-2011 shared task. *ACL HLT 2011*.

D.D. Lewis. 1991. Evaluating text categorization. In *Proc. of Speech and Natural Language Workshop*, pages 312–318.

M.H. MacRoberts and B.R. MacRoberts. 1984. The negational reference: Or the art of dissembling. *Social Studies of Science*, 14(1):91–94.

William C. Mann and Sandra A. Thompson. 1987. Rhetorical Structure Theory: A theory of text organisation. ISI/RS-87-190. Technical report, Information Sciences Institute, University of Southern California, Marina del Rey, CA.

H. Nanba and M. Okumura. 1999. Towards multi-paper summarization using reference information. In *IJCAI*, volume 16, pages 926–931. Citeseer.

V. Ng and C. Cardie. 2002. Improving machine learning approaches to coreference resolution. In *Proc. of ACL*, pages 104–111.

J. O'Connor. 1982. Citing statements: Computer recognition and use to improve retrieval. *Information Processing & Management*, 18(3):125–131.

S.B. Pham and A. Hoffmann. 2004. Extracting positive attributions from scientific papers. In *Discovery Science*, pages 39–45. Springer.

S. Piao, S. Ananiadou, Y. Tsuruoka, Y. Sasaki, and J. McNaught. 2007. Mining opinion polarity relations of citations. In *International Workshop on Computational Semantics (IWCS)*. Citeseer.

L. Polanyi and A. Zaenen. 2006. Contextual valence shifters. *Computing attitude and affect in text: Theory and applications*, pages 1–10.

V. Qazvinian and D.R. Radev. 2008. Scientific paper summarization using citation summary networks. In *Proceedings of the 22nd International Conference on Computational Linguistics-Volume 1*, pages 689–696. Association for Computational Linguistics.

V. Qazvinian and D.R. Radev. 2010. Identifying non-explicit citing sentences for citation-based summarization. In *Proc. of ACL*.

D.R. Radev, M.T. Joseph, B. Gibson, and P. Muthukrishnan. 2009. A Bibliometric and Network Analysis of the field of Computational Linguistics. *Journal of the American Soc. for Info. Sci. and Tech.*

A. Ritchie, S. Robertson, and S. Teufel. 2008. Comparing citation contexts for information retrieval. In *Proc. of ACM conference on Information and knowledge management*, pages 213–222. ACM.

W.M. Soon, H.T. Ng, and D.C.Y. Lim. 2001. A machine learning approach to coreference resolution of noun phrases. *Comp. Ling.*, 27(4):521–544.

I. Spiegel-Rosing. 1977. Science studies: Bibliometric and content analysis. *Social Studies of Science*.

K. Sugiyama, T. Kumar, M.Y. Kan, and R.C. Tripathi. 2010. Identifying citing sentences in research papers using supervised learning. In *Information Retrieval & Knowledge Management,(CAMP), 2010 International Conference on*, pages 67–72. IEEE.

S. Teufel, A. Siddharthan, and D. Tidhar. 2006. Automatic classification of citation function. In *Proc. of EMNLP*, pages 103–110.

Simone Teufel. 2010. *The Structure of Scientific Articles: Applications to Citation Indexing and Summarization*. Stanford: CSLI Publications.

P.D. Turney. 2002. Thumbs up or thumbs down?: semantic orientation applied to unsupervised classification of reviews. In *Proc. of ACL*.

W.J. Wilbur, A. Rzhetsky, and H. Shatkay. 2006. New directions in biomedical text annotation: definitions, guidelines and corpus construction. *BMC bioinformatics*, 7(1):356.

H. Yu and V. Hatzivassiloglou. 2003. Towards answering opinion questions: Separating facts from opinions and identifying the polarity of opinion sentences. In *Proc. of EMNLP*, page 136.

Open-domain Anatomical Entity Mention Detection

Tomoko Ohta [1] **Sampo Pyysalo** [1] **Jun'ichi Tsujii** [2] **Sophia Ananiadou** [1]
[1]National Centre for Text Mining and University of Manchester,
Manchester Interdisciplinary Biocentre, 131 Princess Street, Manchester, UK
[2]Microsoft Research Asia, Beijing, China
okap.tiffany@gmail.com, sampo.pyysalo@gmail.com
jtsujii@microsoft.com, sophia.ananiadou@manchester.ac.uk

Abstract

Anatomical entities such as *kidney*, *muscle* and *blood* are central to much of biomedical scientific discourse, and the detection of mentions of anatomical entities is thus necessary for the automatic analysis of the structure of domain texts. Although a number of resources and methods addressing aspects of the task have been introduced, there have so far been no annotated corpora for training and evaluating systems for broad-coverage, open-domain anatomical entity mention detection. We introduce the AnEM corpus, a domain- and species-independent resource manually annotated for anatomical entity mentions using a fine-grained classification system. The corpus texts are selected randomly from citation abstracts and full-text papers with the aim of making the corpus representative of the entire available biomedical scientific literature. We demonstrate the use of the corpus through an evaluation of the broad-coverage MetaMap tagger and a CRF-based system trained on the corpus data, considering also a combination of these two methods. The combined system demonstrates a promising level of performance, approaching 80% F-score for mention detection for a relaxed matching criterion. The corpus and other introduced resources are available under open licences from `http://www.nactem.ac.uk/anatomy/`.

1 Introduction

Entity mention detection is a prerequisite for most efforts to systematically analyse and represent the structure of scientific discourse. In the life sciences, a comprehensive analysis must include entities at multiple levels of biological organization, from the molecular to the organism level. The detection of references to *anatomical entities* such as "*kidney*" and "*blood*" is thus required for the automatic structured analysis of biomedical scientific text.

Although a wealth of lexical and ontological resources covering anatomical entities are available (Rosse and Mejino, 2003; Smith et al., 2007; Bodenreider, 2004; Haendel et al., 2009), such resources do not alone confer the ability to reliably detect mentions of anatomical entities in natural language (Gerner et al., 2010a; Travillian et al., 2011; Pyysalo et al., 2012b). To support the development and evaluation of reliable anatomical entity mention detection methods, corpus resources annotated specifically for the task are necessary.

In this study, we aim to create a reference standard for evaluating methods for anatomical entity mention detection and for training machine learning-based methods for the task. We seek to select a set of texts that are representative of the relevant scientific literature, i.e. *open-domain* in the sense of avoiding bias toward, for example, specific species, levels of biological organization (e.g. subcellular or gross anatomy), parts of documents (e.g. abstracts), or subdomains of life science. In support of our annotation, we draw on a granularity-based, species-independent upper-level ontology of anatomy as well as relevant species-specific ontological resources.

The overall aim of our efforts is to create methods and resources for comprehensive event-based analysis (Ananiadou et al., 2010) of biomedical scientific discourse involving anatomy-level entities and processes. In aiming to establish a stable basis for anatomical entity mention detection, the present study is an important step toward this goal.

		Label	Ontology classes	Examples
Anatomical entity	Anatomical structure	ORGANISM SUBDIVISION	`organism subdivision`$_{\text{CARO}}$	*head, limb*
		ANATOMICAL SYSTEM	`anatomical system`$_{\text{CARO}}$	*vascular system*
		ORGAN	`compound organ`$_{\text{CARO}}$	*liver, heart*
		MULTI-TISSUE STRUCTURE	`multi-tissue structure`$_{\text{CARO}}$	*artery*
		TISSUE	`portion of tissue`$_{\text{CARO}}$	*epithelium*
		CELL	`cell`$_{\text{CARO}}$	*epithelial cell*
		DEVELOPING ANATOMICAL STRUCTURE	`developing anatomical structure`$_{\text{UBERON}}$	*embryo*
		CELLULAR COMPONENT	`cellular component`$_{\text{GO}}$	*mitochondrion*
		ORGANISM SUBSTANCE	`portion of organism substance`$_{\text{CARO}}$	*blood*
		IMMATERIAL ANATOMICAL ENTITY	`immaterial anatomical entity`$_{\text{CARO}}$	*lumen*
		PATHOLOGICAL FORMATION	–	*carcinoma*

Table 1: Annotations targets with applied label, corresponding ontology classes, and common examples.

2 Corpus Annotation

2.1 Ontological Basis

Following our previous efforts on anatomical entity classification (Pyysalo et al., 2012b), we base our definition of annotated mention scope, the subdivision of anatomical entities into classes, and the class labels applied in our annotation primarily on the Common Anatomy Reference Ontology (CARO) (Haendel et al., 2008). CARO is a small, species-independent ontology of anatomical entities based on the upper-level structure of the Foundational Model of Anatomy (FMA) ontology of human anatomy (Rosse and Mejino, 2003; Rosse and Mejino, 2008). CARO has been proposed as a standard for unifying the upper-level structure of the various existing species-specific ontologies and is adopted by many of the over 40 ontologies involving the anatomy domain in the Open Biomedical Ontologies (OBO) foundry[1] (Smith et al., 2007). CARO adheres to disjoint classes and single inheritance, and divides anatomical structures primarily by granularity (Kumar et al., 2004), a systematic notion familiar to those working in the life sciences.

Although we draw primarily on CARO, we follow the well-established cellular component subontology of the Gene Ontology (GO) (Ashburner et al., 2000) in grouping sub-cellular structures under a single upper-level category. For developing structures that resist granularity-based categorization due to occupying different levels at different stages of development, we adopt a separate DEVELOPING ANATOMICAL STRUCTURE category, as done also in e.g. Uberon (Haendel et al., 2009).

[1]`http://obofoundry.org/`

2.2 Annotation Scope

We diverge from the scope of anatomy ontologies in two important aspects in our annotation.

First, ontologies of anatomy commonly incorporate everything from molecules to whole organisms within their scope. However, in entity mention detection, many molecular level anatomical entities fall within the scope of the established gene/protein mention detection tasks (e.g. (Kim et al., 2004; Tanabe et al., 2005)), and whole organism mentions similarly largely within what is covered by existing methods and resources for organism mention detection (Gerner et al., 2010b; Naderi et al., 2011). To avoid overlap with established tasks and to focus on the novel aspects of anatomical entity mention detection, we exclude biological macromolecules and mentions of organism names from the scope of our annotation, as argued in (Pyysalo et al., 2012b).

Second, these ontologies typically represent *canonical* anatomy, an idealized state that is rarely (if ever) encountered in reality (Bada and Hunter, 2011). As our annotation is intended to cover references to real-world anatomy, we explicitly include in the scope of our annotation also healthy as well as pathological variants of canonical anatomy. We include also entities derived from these anatomical entities through (planned) processing such as surgical or laboratory procedures, even when these processed entities are no longer properly part of the original organism. Finally, we annotate pathological formations such as scars and carcinomas that are part of individual organisms but have no correspondence in canonical anatomy (Smith et al., 2005).

Table 1 presents the class labels applied in the annotation with the corresponding ontology classes.

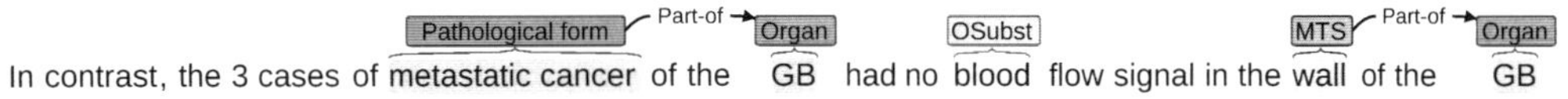

Figure 1: Example sentence with annotation. OSUBST and MTS abbreviate for ORGANISM SUBSTANCE and MULTI-TISSUE STRUCTURE, respectively.

2.3 Representation

The primary corpus annotation marks mentions of anatomical entities as contiguous spans of characters in text, each of which is assigned a type (Figure 1). As the CARO-based categorization has comprehensive coverage and disjoint classes, each annotation can be assigned exactly one type (class label).

In addition to identifying and typing anatomical entity mentions, we further apply binary attributes ("flags") marking the following characteristics of each mention:

DEVELOPING developing variant of anatomical entity, e.g. *fetal liver*

PATHOLOGICAL pathological variant of anatomical entity, e.g. *carcinoma cell*

PLANT anatomical entity that is part of a plant (member of the *Viridiplantae* kingdom), e.g. *roots, leaf*

PROCESSED variant of anatomical entity that has undergone planned processing, e.g. *tissue specimen*

Any combination of attributes can apply to a single mention. These attributes allow the identification of subsets of annotations that may be out of scope for some efforts (e.g. pathological or processed entities) and facilitate the analysis of mention detection system performance by identifying particular problematic categories.

2.4 Annotation Criteria

In very brief summary, we annotate spans of text that refer to anatomical entities as defined above. Mentions that involve only metaphorical senses of such entities ("*on the other* hand") or artificial analogues ("*artificial* heart") are not annotated.

The primary targets of our annotation are anatomical entity names (e.g. "*lymphocyte*") and nominal mentions of anatomical entities (e.g. "*muscle tissue*"). Both names and nominal mentions are annotated similarly, without distinction. We exclude pronouns (*it*, *that*) from annotation even when they unambiguously refer to an anatomical entity; we consider the identification and resolution of such mentions part of the distinct coreference resolution task (see e.g. Pradhan et al. (2011)).

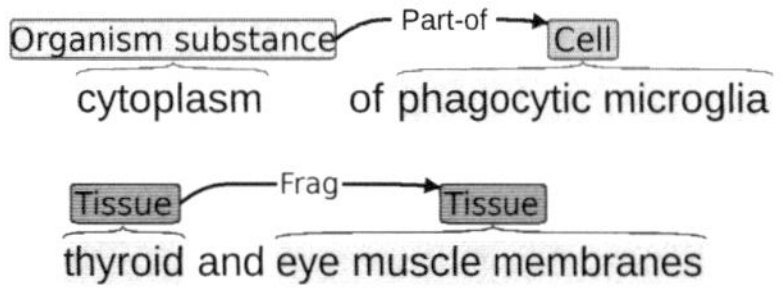

Figure 2: Part-of relation marking entity mention spanning a prepositional phrase (above) and Frag relation marking coordination with ellipsis (below).

In addition to names and nominal mentions, we mark adjectives that have an unambiguous sense of relating to a specific anatomical entity. Thus, for example, both "*kidney*" and "*renal*" (relating to the kidneys) are annotated as ORGAN in expressions such as "*kidney failure*" and "*renal failure*". The choice to annotate adjectival references is motivated by the expected needs of applications making use of automatically detected anatomical entity mentions. For example, for semantic search targeting documents relating to organ failure, a document discussing "*renal failure*" is obviously relevant and should be recovered.

Syntactically, annotations mainly cover base noun phrases without determiners, i.e. nouns with premodifiers relevant to identifying the specific anatomical entity referred to. We exclude noun phrase postmodifiers such as prepositional phrases from the span of single annotations, but apply a separate level of annotation for *part-of* relations that allow such alternate spans to be recovered when they identify an anatomical entity (Figure 2 top). Similarly, we decompose coordinated references to anatomical entities involving ellipsis to non-overlapping spans, but mark the cases using a *frag*(*ment*) relation type (Figure 2 bottom). (Due to space considerations, we omit detailed discussion of these relation annotations.) Together with the properties described in Section 2.3, these constraints assure that any single token is assigned at most one class label and allow the annotation to be repre-

Task	Strict	Matching criterion Left boundary	Right boundary
Mention detection (single class)	89.2%/ 82.0%/ 85.4%	93.0%/ 85.5%/ 89.1%	94.6%/ 86.9%/ 90.6%
Detection and classification (multi-class)	85.6%/ 78.7%/ 82.0%	87.0%/ 80.0%/ 83.3%	90.2%/ 82.9%/ 86.4%

Table 2: Inter-annotator agreement results (precision / recall / F-score).

sented in the standard BIO format and to be straightforwardly applied with many existing entity mention taggers.

By contrast to previously introduced domain resources for e.g. molecular entity and organism mention detection (Tanabe et al., 2005; Gerner et al., 2010b), we do not incorporate any specificity constraints in our annotation criteria. That is, non-specific expressions such as "*tissue*" and "*organ*" are marked identically to specific ones such as "*epithelium*" and "*heart*". This choice seeks to assure the generality of the task and methods for addressing it.

2.5 Text Selection

Texts for the corpus were drawn from two sources: the PubMed[2] database of publication abstracts, and the PubMed Central[3] (PMC) Open Access subset of full-text publications. PubMed, containing more than 20 million citations, has a very broad coverage of domain scientific texts but is limited to publication abstracts, while PMC has lower coverage but does provide over 400,000 full-text documents under open licenses. By sampling both sources, we seek to assure the corpus is relevant to IE efforts regardless of their choice of texts.

To avoid bias toward e.g. subdomains of biology or specific species, we selected texts from both sources by random sampling. For PubMed, we simply selected a random set of citations and extracted their abstract and title texts. For PMC, we initially extracted all non-overlapping section texts (PMC XML `<sec>` elements) as well as caption texts (`<caption>` elements), and then selected a random set of extracts. This selection seeks to maximize the diversity of the texts in the full-text section of the corpus, and the selection of extracts larger than isolated sentences aims to allow the corpus to be used to study methods making use of broader context, e.g. by incorporating constraints such as one sense per discourse (Gale et al., 1992).

We selected a total of 500 documents using this protocol, half from PubMed and half from PMC document extracts. (Descriptive statistics of the *abstracts* and *full-text extracts* subcorpora are given later in Table 3.)

2.6 Annotation Process

Primary annotation was created by a PhD biologist with extensive experience in domain information extraction and text annotation (TO). The use of any relevant resources, such as the full article being annotated or species-specific anatomy ontologies in the OBO foundry, was encouraged for resolving unclear or ambiguous cases during annotation. Initial annotation was produced entirely manually. To further assure the quality of the annotation, a series of automatic tests was performed and used as the basis of a further manual round of revision.[4] Annotation guidelines were initially created based on those created by our previous domain-specific effort (Pyysalo et al., 2012a) and revised throughout the annotation effort to document specific decisions made during annotation. The annotations were created using the BRAT annotation tool (Stenetorp et al., 2012).

To evaluate the annotation consistency, we performed an inter-annotator agreement (IAA) experiment. After brief training with annotation guidelines provided by the primary annotator, a random 10% of the corpus was independently annotated by a PhD computer scientist with experience in domain text annotation and anatomy ontologies (SP). IAA was evaluated using the same criteria as applied in experiments (see Section 3.4), holding the primary annotation as gold. The results are shown in Table 2. We find very good agreement both for mention detection (ignoring classification) as well as for the full task, indicating that the task is well defined and the annotation consistency high.

[2] `http://pubmed.com`

[3] `http://www.ncbi.nlm.nih.gov/pmc/`

[4] No automatically suggested annotations were incorporated into the corpus without manual verification.

3 Methods

We next present the methods applied in our anatomical entity mention detection experiments. We aim to evaluate the capacity of the newly annotated corpus to support reliable mention detection and to establish initial baseline results for the newly introduced resource, and thus focus only on relatively straightforward applications of existing methods.

3.1 MetaMap

MetaMap[5] (Aronson, 2001) is a tool capable of detecting mentions of concepts from the extensive UMLS Metathesaurus (Bodenreider, 2004) in text. The metathesaurus and MetaMap have broad coverage of concepts relevant to biology and medicine and provide a categorization of concepts into 133 semantic types, ranging from `Amino Acid` to `Health Care Activity` to `Vertebrate`, many directly relevant to anatomical entities. MetaMap is a key component of the process used by the National Library of Medicine (NLM) to index publications in the PubMed database and has been applied in numerous other information extraction and information retrieval tasks (Aronson and Lang, 2010).

In initial experiments, we applied MetaMap to training set documents to identify the subset of the 133 semantic classes relevant to anatomy, selecting 14 classes (including e.g. `Cell`, `Tissue` and `Body Substance`) for final experiments.[6] During testing, we used command-line arguments to restrict output to the selected semantic classes. The core tagging functionality of MetaMap is rule-based, and it does not support training on tagged data for concept mention detection. With the exception of the semantic class selection, the evaluation of MetaMap reflects an "off-the-shelf" application of the general-purpose tool.

3.2 CRF tagging

Conditional Random Fields (CRF) (Lafferty et al., 2001) are graphical models that are frequently applied to sequence labeling tasks, and CRFs form the basis of state-of-the-art methods for many entity mention tagging tasks. We performed experiments using the NERsuite entity mention recognition toolkit, based on the CRFsuite implementation of CRFs (Okazaki, 2007). NERsuite provides an extensive set of features applied in entity mention detection, allowing the tool to achieve performance competitive with state-of-the-art methods for many biomedical domain tasks through retraining without task-specific adaptation[7]. Retraining the tool for new tasks is also straightforward, allowing application to new tasks with modest effort.

We set the L_2 regularization parameter of the learning method using held-out evaluation with training set data, picking out of a set of values 2^n ($n \in \mathbb{Z}$) the one giving best performance.[8] Other learning method parameters were left at default values.

3.3 System combination

As a third system, we apply a straightforward combination of the MetaMap and CRF tagging systems, where we initially tag the data using MetaMap and then incorporate the classes assigned by MetaMap as features for training and testing with NERsuite (stacking). More specifically, we create a BIO-tagged version of MetaMap output segmented to match NERsuite tokenization, and assign each token the BIO tag based on the MetaMap semantic type code (e.g. `B-cell`) as a feature.

Excepting for the addition of these MetaMap-derived features, NERsuite is applied as described above (Section 3.2).

3.4 Experimental setting

We split the corpus data into two primary parts: a training set consisting of 60% of the documents and a test set of the remaining 40%. The data splits were performed independently for the two subcorpora (abstracts and full-text extracts), using stratified sampling to assure broadly comparable statistical properties between the sets. The test set was held out during development and only applied for the final experiments.

[5] `http://metamap.nlm.nih.gov/`

[6] In brief, we tagged the training data with MetaMap, extracted the subset of semantic classes giving more than 5% precision against the gold annotations, and manually analysed these to select this subset. The selected classes are detailed in supplementary material available on the project webpage.

[7] `http://nersuite.nlplab.org/`

[8] Specifically, $C_2 = 2^{-5}$ was selected.

Source	Item	Dataset Train	Test	Total
Abst.	Document	150	100	250
	Word	28,960	18,199	47,159
	Entity	1,182	764	1,946
FTE	Document	150	100	250
	Word	26,306	17,955	44,261
	Entity	697	492	1,189
Total	Document	300	200	500
	Word	55,266	36,154	91,420
	Entity	1,879	1,256	3,135

Table 3: Overall corpus statistics. Statistics given separately for the abstracts (abst.) and full-text extracts (FTE) subcorpora as well as for the total.

Type	Count
CELL	776
MULTI-TISSUE STRUCTURE	639
ORGAN	381
PATHOLOGICAL FORMATION	368
ORGANISM SUBSTANCE	291
CELLULAR COMPONENT	199
TISSUE	169
ORGANISM SUBDIVISION	162
IMMATERIAL ANATOMICAL ENTITY	60
ANATOMICAL SYSTEM	51
DEVELOPING ANATOMICAL STRUCTURE	39

Table 4: Annotation statistics by type.

We perform experiments in two settings: a single-class setting where the task is restricted to the detection of anatomical entity mentions without classification, and a multi-class setting where the correct class label must further be assigned to each detected mention. As MetaMap uses UMLS semantic classes that do not fully align with the applied CARO-based classes, MetaMap is only applied in the single-class setting.

For evaluation, we adopted the protocol, criteria and metrics of the established BioNLP/JNLPBA shared task 2004 (Kim et al., 2004). To assure compatibility, we created our evaluation tool on the basis of the shared task evaluation script. The evaluation is thus based on entity-wise (microaverage) precision/recall/F-score metrics, and tagging performance is separately evaluated under *strict match*, *left boundary match* and *right boundary match* criteria. In the former setting, a predicted entity must exactly match the extent of a gold standard entity, while in the latter two settings, it is enough that the left/right boundary matches.

3.5 Format

The annotation is distributed in the standard column-based BIO format applied for e.g. CoNLL 2003 (Tjong Kim Sang and De Meulder, 2003) and JNLPBA (Kim et al., 2004) data, among other established datasets.

4 Results

4.1 Corpus statistics

Table 3 presents the overall corpus statistics. We note that the abstracts and full-text extracts (FTE) subcorpora are of comparable size in terms of their word counts, but the number of annotations is 1.6 times higher in the abstracts subcorpus (1.5 correcting for number of words). This difference in anatomical entity mention density between abstracts and full texts parallels the findings of Cohen et al. (2010) on the relative density of gene, drug and disease mentions. We further note that the estimated density of anatomical entity mentions in abstracts (approx. 41 per 1000 words) and full texts (27 per 1000) are broadly comparable to the gene mention density estimates of Cohen et al. (61 and 47 for abstracts and full texts, respectively).

Table 4 presents a breakdown by annotation type. There are large differences in the number of annotations by type, with the majority class CELL outnumbering the rarest type 20-fold. While the total number of annotated examples is likely to be sufficient for training machine learning-based taggers and most of the classes contain a respectable number of examples, the statistics suggest that the least frequently annotated types may represent challenges for learning.

4.2 Entity Mention Detection

Table 5 presents the experimental results for anatomical entity mention detection (single-class). In terms of F-score, we find the same ranking of the three methods for all three criteria, with the CRF-based tagger outperforming the rule-based MetaMap, and the combination method outperforming its components. Although it is not surprising that a dedicated machine learning-based system is capable of outperforming a general-purpose, largely rule-based system, this result does reflect positively on both the

Method	Matching criterion Strict	Left boundary	Right boundary
MetaMap	50.78% / 64.49% / 56.82%	54.67% / 69.43% / 61.17%	58.18% / 73.89% / 65.10%
NERsuite	77.98% / 52.15% / 62.50%	81.43% / 54.46% / 65.27%	90.00% / 60.19% / 72.14%
MetaMap + NERsuite	82.09% / 62.42% / 70.92%	84.61% / 64.33% / 73.09%	90.68% / 68.95% / 78.34%

Table 5: Overall single-class anatomical entity mention detection results (precision / recall / F-score).

Method	Matching criterion Strict	Left boundary	Right boundary
NERsuite	72.07% / 42.12% / 53.17%	72.75% / 42.52% / 53.67%	85.69% / 50.08% / 63.22%
MetaMap + NERsuite	75.41% / 51.75% / 61.38%	76.45% / 52.47% / 62.23%	83.99% / 57.64% / 68.37%

Table 6: Overall anatomical entity mention detection and classification results (precision / recall / F-score).

consistency of the annotation as well as the sufficiency of the size of the newly introduced corpus. In this application, we find that MetaMap tends to favor recall over precision – perhaps reflecting its focus on IR applications (Aronson and Lang, 2010) – while the trained machine learning-based models are clearly biased in favor of high precision.

As expected on the basis of the results of previous evaluations using similar experimental setups (Kim et al., 2004), results are notably better under the relaxed matching criteria. In particular, requiring only the right boundaries of annotations to match yields F-scores nearly 10% points higher than under strict matching. Recalling that the annotations primarily mark base noun phrases, this suggests that the systems comparatively frequently identify the head word of an anatomical entity mention correctly but differ from gold annotation regarding the choice of premodifiers included in the span of the annotation. As limited variation in premodifier selection is arguably acceptable for many applications and relaxed matching criteria are frequently applied in domain tagging tasks (Kim et al., 2004; Wilbur et al., 2007), we propose to consider performance under the relaxed *right boundary match* criterion as the primary result for evaluation using the new corpus.

Table 6 presents the results for anatomical entity mention detection and classification using the 11-class categorization used in annotation.[9] While performance in terms of F-score is approximately 10% points lower than for the single-class task, this drop is comparatively modest given the large number of distinct classes, indicating that the number of annotations of most individual classes is sufficient for learning.

While these initial results are not as high as for established entity mention detection tasks in the domain (Wilbur et al., 2007; Rebholz-Schuhmann et al., 2011), we consider the level of performance quite good given the many new challenges relating to the task. Further, as the mention detection methods were also applied with only modest specific adaptation to the task, we believe there remain many opportunities for further development of methods for the task.

4.3 Discussion

Many commonly targeted mention types in both the "general" and the biological domain are frequently characterized by obvious surface features: the names of people and locations are capitalized in many languages, as are genera in scientific species' names, and many gene and chemical names have comparable features distinguishing them from common nouns (consider e.g. *p53*, *IgE*, *c-myc*, *Ca2+*, *H2SO4*). By contrast, many typical anatomical entity mentions are common noun compounds lacking obvious distinguishing surface features. This fact likely contributes to the comparatively low performance of the CRF-based tagger when applied without support from lexical resources.

A further challenge that arises comparatively frequently in anatomical entity mention detection is ambiguity between entity mentions and other words sharing the same surface form. For example, while *Barack Obama*, *Sweden*, *p53* and *H2SO4* can be

[9] Note that evaluation using MetaMap only is not possible as its semantic classes differ from those used in the annotation.

safely identified as mentions of a person, country, gene, and chemical without reference to context, *face* should not be marked as an anatomical entity mention in *face the facts*, nor should *Airways* in *British Airways*. Thus, approaches relying on simple matching against lexical resources will not suffice for accurate anatomical entity mention detection.

Our evaluation results demonstrated a clear advantage to combining detection based on lexical resources with machine learning-based tagging, an approach we believe will be key to the further development of reliable anatomical entity mention tagging that we will seek to explore in detail in future work. To facilitate analysis of the performance of the methods, we provide the predictions of each method in supplementary data on the project homepage.

5 Related work

A number of domain corpora such as GENIA (Ohta et al., 2002), BioInfer (Pyysalo et al., 2007), and the recently introduced CellFinder corpus (Neves et al., 2012) include annotation for at least some classes of anatomical entities. However, such corpora typically cover only specific subdomains of the literature, such as transcription factors in human blood cells (GENIA), protein-protein interactions (BioInfer), or stem cells (CellFinder). To the best of our knowledge, this is the first effort introducing a corpus annotated for anatomical entity mentions that specifically aims to be representative of the entire available literature. We note that there is a well-established precedent to this goal: sentences for the *de facto* standard corpus for gene/protein name recognition, GENETAG (Tanabe et al., 2005), were similarly selected from PubMed abstracts without domain restrictions.

The BioNLP/JNLPBA shared task 2004 (Kim et al., 2004) targeted the detection of mentions of five types of biological entities, including two that would fall within in the scope of our CELL annotation ("Cell type" and "Cell line"). Other than this comparatively early shared task, collaborative domain efforts such as BioCreative (Krallinger et al., 2008) and CALBC (Rebholz-Schuhmann et al., 2011) have not targeted anatomical entity mentions.

Some recent studies have considered the use of ontological resources for the detection of anatomical entity mentions in natural language expressions. In previous work (Pyysalo et al., 2012b), we studied the classification of isolated noun phrases extracted from PubMed to identify anatomy terms. Travillian et al. (2011) considered two lexical matching applications to detect anatomical entities from two OBO resources in user-provided terms. However, these efforts have not involved the annotation or detection of mentions in context, which we view as critical for real-world entity mention detection method development and evaluation.

6 Conclusions

We have introduced a manually annotated corpus for open-domain anatomical entity mention detection, consisting of 500 documents (over 90,000 words) drawn from publication abstracts and full texts. The primary corpus annotation consists of the identification of over 3,000 references to both healthy and pathological anatomical entities, marked using a detailed 11-class categorization based on established biomedical domain ontologies. We demonstrated the use of the new corpus through a comparative evaluation of MetaMap, a general semantic class tagger; NERsuite, a CRF-based machine learning system; and a stacked combination of the two, finding that under a relaxed matching criterion, the combination approaches 80% F-score at mention detection and 70% F-score at mention detection and classification. This level of performance is encouraging for a first application and suggests that reliable open-domain anatomical entity mention detection is not an unrealistic target.

We hope that the introduced corpus can serve as a reference standard for the further development and evaluation of methods for anatomical entity mention detection. This corpus, the introduced evaluation tools, and other resources created in this study are made available under open licences from `http://www.nactem.ac.uk/anatomy/`.

Acknowledgments

This work was funded by UK Biotechnology and Biological Sciences Research Council (BBSRC) under project Automated Biological Event Extraction from the Literature for Drug Discovery (reference number: BB/G013160/1).

References

S. Ananiadou, S. Pyysalo, J. Tsujii, and D.B. Kell. 2010. Event extraction for systems biology by text mining the literature. *Trends in Biotechnology*, 28(7):381–390.

A.R. Aronson and F.M. Lang. 2010. An overview of MetaMap: historical perspective and recent advances. *Journal of the American Medical Informatics Association*, 17(3):229–236.

A.R. Aronson. 2001. Effective mapping of biomedical text to the UMLS Metathesaurus: the MetaMap program. In *Proceedings of AMIA*, pages 17–21.

M Ashburner, CA Ball, JA Blake, D Botstein, H Butler, JM Cherry, AP Davis, K Dolinski, SS Dwight, JT Eppig, MA Harris, DP Hill, L Issel-Tarver, A Kasarskis, S Lewis, JC Matese, JE Richardson, M Ringwald, GM Rubin, and G Sherlock. 2000. Gene ontology: tool for the unification of biology. *Nature genetics*, 25:25–29.

M. Bada and L. Hunter. 2011. Desiderata for ontologies to be used in semantic annotation of biomedical documents. *Journal of Biomedical Informatics*, 44(1):94–101.

O. Bodenreider. 2004. The unified medical language system (UMLS): integrating biomedical terminology. *Nucleic acids research*, 32(suppl 1):D267–D270.

K.B. Cohen, H. Johnson, K. Verspoor, C. Roeder, and L. Hunter. 2010. The structural and content aspects of abstracts versus bodies of full text journal articles are different. *BMC bioinformatics*, 11(1):492.

W.A. Gale, K.W. Church, and D. Yarowsky. 1992. One sense per discourse. In *Proceedings of the workshop on Speech and Natural Language*, pages 233–237.

M. Gerner, G. Nenadic, and C.M. Bergman. 2010a. An exploration of mining gene expression mentions and their anatomical locations from biomedical text. In *BioNLP'10*, pages 72–80.

M. Gerner, G. Nenadic, and C.M. Bergman. 2010b. LINNAEUS: a species name identification system for biomedical literature. *BMC bioinformatics*, 11(1):85+.

M.A. Haendel, F. Neuhaus, D. Osumi-Sutherland, P.M. Mabee, J.L.V. Mejino, C.J. Mungall, and B. Smith. 2008. CARO–the common anatomy reference ontology. *Anatomy Ontologies for Bioinformatics*, pages 327–349.

M.A. Haendel, G.G. Gkoutos, S.E. Lewis, and C. Mungall. 2009. Uberon: towards a comprehensive multi-species anatomy ontology. *Nature precedings*.

J-D. Kim, T. Ohta, Y. Tsuruoka, Y. Tateisi, and N. Collier. 2004. Introduction to the bio-entity recognition task at JNLPBA. In *Proceedings JNLPBA'04*.

M. Krallinger, A. Morgan, L. Smith, F. Leitner, L. Tanabe, J. Wilbur, L. Hirschman, and A. Valencia. 2008. Evaluation of text-mining systems for biology: overview of the Second BioCreative community challenge. *Genome biology*, 9(Suppl 2):S1.

A. Kumar, B. Smith, and D.D. Novotny. 2004. Biomedical informatics and granularity. *Comparative and functional genomics*, 5(6-7):501–508.

J.D. Lafferty, A. McCallum, and F.C.N. Pereira. 2001. Conditional random fields: Probabilistic models for segmenting and labeling sequence data. In *Proceedings of ICML*, pages 282–289.

N. Naderi, T. Kappler, C.J.O. Baker, and R. Witte. 2011. OrganismTagger: Detection, normalization, and grounding of organism entities in biomedical documents. *Bioinformatics*.

M. Neves, A. Damaschun, A. Kurtz, and U. Leser. 2012. Annotating and evaluating text for stem cell research. In *Third Workshop on Building and Evaluation Resources for Biomedical Text Mining (BioTxtM 2012)*. (to appear).

T Ohta, Y Tateisi, H Mima, and J Tsujii. 2002. GENIA corpus: an annotated research abstract corpus in molecular biology domain. *Proceedings of the Human Language Technology Conference (HLT 2002)*, pages 73–77.

N. Okazaki. 2007. CRFsuite: a fast implementation of conditional random fields (CRFs). http://www.chokkan.org/software/crfsuite/.

S. Pradhan, L. Ramshaw, M. Marcus, M. Palmer, R. Weischedel, and N. Xue. 2011. CoNLL-2011 shared task: Modeling unrestricted coreference in ontonotes. In *Proceedings of the Fifteenth Conference on Computational Natural Language Learning: Shared Task*, pages 1–27.

S. Pyysalo, F. Ginter, J. Heimonen, J. Björne, J. Boberg, J. Järvinen, and T. Salakoski. 2007. BioInfer: A corpus for information extraction in the biomedical domain. *BMC Bioinformatics*, 8(50).

S. Pyysalo, T. Ohta, M. Miwa, H-C. Cho, J. Tsujii, and S. Ananiadou. 2012a. Event extraction across multiple levels of biological organization. (manuscript in review).

S. Pyysalo, T. Ohta, J. Tsujii, and S. Ananiadou. 2012b. Learning to classify anatomical entities using open biomedical ontologies. *Journal of Biomedical Semantics*. (to appear).

D. Rebholz-Schuhmann, A. Yepes, C. Li, S. Kafkas, I. Lewin, N. Kang, P. Corbett, D. Milward, E. Buyko, E. Beisswanger, K. Hornbostel, A. Kouznetsov, R. Witte, J. Laurila, C. Baker, C. Kuo, S. Clematide, F. Rinaldi, R. Farkas, G. Mora, K. Hara, L.I. Furlong, M. Rautschka, M. Neves, A. Pascual-Montano,

Q. Wei, N. Collier, M. Chowdhury, A. Lavelli, R. Berlanga, R. Morante, V. Van Asch, W. Daelemans, J. Marina, E. van Mulligen, J. Kors, and U. Hahn. 2011. Assessment of NER solutions against the first and second calbc silver standard corpus. *Journal of Biomedical Semantics*, 2(Suppl 5):S11.

C. Rosse and J.L.V. Mejino. 2003. A reference ontology for biomedical informatics: the foundational model of anatomy. *Journal of Biomedical Informatics*, 36(6):478–500.

C. Rosse and J.L.V. Mejino. 2008. The foundational model of anatomy ontology. *Anatomy Ontologies for Bioinformatics*, pages 59–117.

B. Smith, A. Kumar, W. Ceusters, and C. Rosse. 2005. On carcinomas and other pathological entities. *Comparative and functional genomics*, 6(7-8):379–387.

B. Smith, M. Ashburner, C. Rosse, J. Bard, W. Bug, W. Ceusters, L. J Goldberg, K. Eilbeck, A. Ireland, C.J. Mungall, N. Leontis, P. Rocca-Serra, A. Ruttenberg, S-A Sansone, R.H. Scheuermann, N. Shah, P.L. Whetzel, and S. Lewis. 2007. The OBO Foundry: coordinated evolution of ontologies to support biomedical data integration. *Nature biotechnology*, 25(11):1251–1255.

P. Stenetorp, S. Pyysalo, G. Topić, T. Ohta, S. Ananiadou, and J. Tsujii. 2012. brat: a web-based tool for NLP-assisted text annotation. In *Proceedings of the EACL 2012 Demonstrations*, pages 102–107.

L. Tanabe, N. Xie, L. Thom, W. Matten, and W.J. Wilbur. 2005. GENETAG: a tagged corpus for gene/protein named entity recognition. *BMC bioinformatics*, 6(Suppl 1):S3.

E.F. Tjong Kim Sang and F. De Meulder. 2003. Introduction to the CoNLL-2003 shared task: Language-independent named entity recognition. In *Proceedings of the seventh conference on Natural language learning at HLT-NAACL 2003*, pages 142–147.

R. Travillian, T. Adamusiak, T. Burdett, M. Gruenberger, J. Hancock, A-M. Mallon, J. Malone, P. Schofield, and H. Parkinson. 2011. Anatomy ontologies and potential users: bridging the gap. *Journal of Biomedical Semantics*, 2(Suppl 4):S3.

J. Wilbur, L. Smith, and L. Tanabe. 2007. BioCreative 2 Gene Mention Task. In *Proceedings of Second BioCreative Challenge Evaluation Workshop*, pages 7–16.

A Three-Way Perspective on Scientific Discourse Annotation for Knowledge Extraction

Maria Liakata
Aberystwyth University, UK /
EMBL-EBI, UK
liakata@ebi.ac.uk

Paul Thompson
University of Manchester, UK
paul.thompson@manchester.ac.uk

Anita de Waard
Elsevier Labs, USA /
UiL-OTS, Universiteit Utrecht, NL
a.dewaard@elsevier.com

Raheel Nawaz
University of Manchester, UK
raheel.nawaz@cs.man.ac.uk

Henk Pander Maat
UiL-OTS, Universiteit Utrecht, NL
h.l.w.pandermaat@uu.nl

Sophia Ananiadou
University of Manchester, UK
sophia.ananiadou@manchester.ac.uk

Abstract

This paper presents a three-way perspective on the annotation of discourse in scientific literature. We use three different schemes, each of which focusses on different aspects of discourse in scientific articles, to annotate a corpus of three full-text papers, and compare the results. One scheme seeks to identify the core components of scientific investigations at the sentence level, a second annotates meta-knowledge pertaining to bio-events and a third considers how epistemic knowledge is conveyed at the clause level. We present our analysis of the comparison, and a discussion of the contributions of each scheme.

1 Introduction

The literature boom in the life sciences over the past few years has sparked increasing interest into text mining tools, which facilitate the automatic extraction of useful knowledge from text (Ananiadou et al., 2006; Ananiadou & McNaught, 2006; Zweigenbaum et al., 2007; Cohen & Hunter, 2008). Most of these tools have focussed on entity recognition and relation extraction and with few exceptions, e.g., (Hyland, 1996; Light et al., 2004; Sándor, 2007; Vincze et al., 2008), do not take into account the discourse context of the knowledge extracted. However, failure to take this context into account results in the loss of information vital for the correct interpretation of extracted knowledge, e.g. the scope of the relations, or the level of certainty with which they are expressed. A particular piece of knowledge may represent, e.g., an accepted fact, hypothesis, results of an experiment, analysis based on experimental results, factual or speculative statements etc. Furthermore, this knowledge may represent the author's current work, or work reported elsewhere. The ability to recognise different discourse elements automatically provides crucial information for the correct interpretation of extracted knowledge, allowing scientific claims to be linked to experimental evidence, or newly reported experimental knowledge to be isolated. The importance of categorising such knowledge becomes more pronounced as analysis moves from abstracts to full papers, where the content is richer and linguistic constructions are more complex (Cohen et al., 2010). Analysis of full papers is extremely important, since less than 8% of scientific claims occur in abstracts (Blake, 2010).

Various different schemes for annotating discourse elements in scientific texts have been proposed. The schemes vary along several axes, including perspective, motivation, complexity and the granularity of the units of text to which the scheme is applied. Faced with such variety, it is important to be able to select the best scheme(s) for the purpose at hand. Answers to questions such as the following can help in the selection process:

1. What are the relative merits of the different schemes?
2. What are the similarities and differences between schemes?
3. Can annotation according to multiple schemes provide enhanced information?

Category	Description
`Hypothesis`	An unconfirmed statement which is a stepping stone of the investigation
`Motivation`	The reasons behind an investigation
`Background`	Generally accepted background knowledge and previous work
`Goal`	A target state of the investigation where intended discoveries are made
`Object-New`	An entity which is a product or main theme of the investigation
`Object-New-Advantage`	Advantage of an object
`Object-New-Disadvantage`	Disadvantage of an object
`Method-New`	Means by which authors seek to achieve a goal of the investigation
`Method-New-Advantage`	Advantage of a Method
`Method-New-Disadvantage`	Disadvantage of a Method
`Method-Old`	A method mentioned pertaining to previous work
`Method-Old-Advantage`	Advantage of a Method
`Method-Old-Disadvantage`	Disadvantage of a Method
`Experiment`	An experimental method
`Model`	A statement about a theoretical model or framework
`Observation`	The data/phenomena recorded in an investigation
`Result`	Factual statements about the outputs, interpretation of observations
`Conclusion`	Statements inferred from observations & results

Table 1. The CoreSC Annotation scheme: layers 1 & 2

4. Is there any advantage in merging annotation schemes or is it better to allow complementary and different dimensions of scientific discourse annotation?

As a starting point to addressing such questions, we provide a comparison of three different schemes for the annotation of discourse elements within scientific papers. Each scheme has a different perspective and motivation:, one is content-driven, seeking to identify the main components of a scientific investigation, another is driven by the need to describe events of biomedical relevance and the third focusses on how epistemic knowledge is conveyed in discourse.

These different viewpoints mean that the schemes vary in both the type and complexity of the discourse elements identified, as well as the types of units to which the annotation is applied, i.e. complete sentences, segments of sentences, or specific relations/events occurring within these sentences. To facilitate the comparison, we have annotated three full papers according to each of the schemes. The analysis resulting from this three-way annotation considers mappings between schemes, their relative merits, and how the information annotated by the different schemes can complement each other to provide enriched details about knowledge extracted from the texts.

In the following sections, we firstly provide a description of the three schemes, and then explain how they have been used in our corpus annotation. Finally we discuss the results from the comparison, and the features of each scheme.

2 Sentence annotation: CoreSC scheme

The reasoning behind this scheme is that a paper is the human-readable representation of a scientific investigation. Therefore, the goal of the annotation is to retrieve the content model of scientific investigations as reflected within scientific discourse. The hypothesis is that there is a set of core scientific concepts (CoreSC), which constitute the key components of a scientific investigation. CoreSCs consist of 11 concepts originating from the CISP (Core Information about Scientific Papers) meta-data (Soldatova & Liakata, 2007), which are a subset of classes from the EXPO ontology for the description of scientific experiments (Soldatova & King, 2006). The CoreSCs are: *Motivation, Goal, Object, Background, Hypothesis, Method, Model, Experiment, Observation, Result* and *Conclusion.*

The CoreSC scheme (Liakata et al., 2010; Liakata et al., 2012) implements the above-mentioned concepts as a 3-layered sentence-based annotation scheme. This means that each sentence in a document is assigned one of the 11 CoreSC concepts. The scheme also considers a layer designated to properties of the concepts (e.g. New Method vs Old Method) as well as identifiers which link instances of the same concept across sentences. A short definition of CoreSC categories and their properties can be found in Table 1.

The CoreSC scheme is accompanied by 47-page annotation guidelines, and has been used by 16 domain experts to annotate a corpus of 265 full papers from physical chemistry & biochemistry (Liakata & Soldatova, 2009; Liakata et al., 2010). This corpus consists of 40,000 sentences, containing over 1 million words and was developed in three phases (for details see Liakata et al. (2012)). Inter-annotator agreement between experts was measured in terms of Cohen's kappa (Cohen, 1960) on 41 papers and ranged between 0.5 and 0.7. Machine learning classifiers have been trained on the CoreSC corpus, achieving > 51% accuracy across the eleven categories. The most accurately predicted category is *Experiment,* the category describing experimental methods (Liakata et al., 2012). Classifiers trained on 1000 Biology abstracts annotated with CoreSC have obtained an accuracy of over 80% (Guo et al., 2010). Models trained on the CoreSC corpus papers have been used to create automatic summaries of the papers, which have been evaluated in a question answering task (Liakata et al., 2012). Lastly, the CoreSC scheme was used to annotate 50 papers from Pubmed Central pertaining to Cancer Risk Assessment. A web tool (SAPIENTA[1]) allows users to annotate their full papers with Core Scientific concepts, and can be combined with manual annotation. A UIMA framework [2] implementation of this code for large-scale annotation of CoreSC concepts is in progress.

3 Event annotation: Meta-knowledge for bio-events

The motivation for this annotation scheme is to allow the training of more sophisticated event-based information extraction systems. In contrast to the sentence-based scheme described in section 2, this scheme is applied at the level of *events* (Ananiadou et al., 2010), of which there may be several within a single sentence.

3.1 Bio-Events

Events are template-like, structured representations of pieces of knowledge contained within sentences. Normally, events are "anchored" to a *trigger* (typically a verb or noun) around which the knowledge expressed is organised. Each event has one of more participants, which describe different aspects of the event. Participants can correspond to entities or other events, and are often labelled with semantic roles, e.g., CAUSE, THEME, LOCATION, etc. The work described here focusses specifically on bio-events, which are complex structured relations representing fine-grained relations between bio-entities and their modifiers. Figure 1 provides some examples of bio-events. Event extraction systems (Björne et al., 2009; Miwa et al., 2010; Miwa et al., 2012; Quirk et al., 2011) are typically trained on text corpora, in which events and their participants have been manually annotated by domain experts. Research into bio-event extraction has been boosted by the two recent shared tasks at BioNLP 2009/2011 (Kim et al., 2011; Pyysalo et al., In Press). Several gold standard event annotated corpora exist; examples include the GENIA Event Corpus (Kim et al., 2008), GREC (Thompson et al., 2009) and BioInfer (Pyysalo et al., 2007), in addition to the corpora produced for the shared tasks.

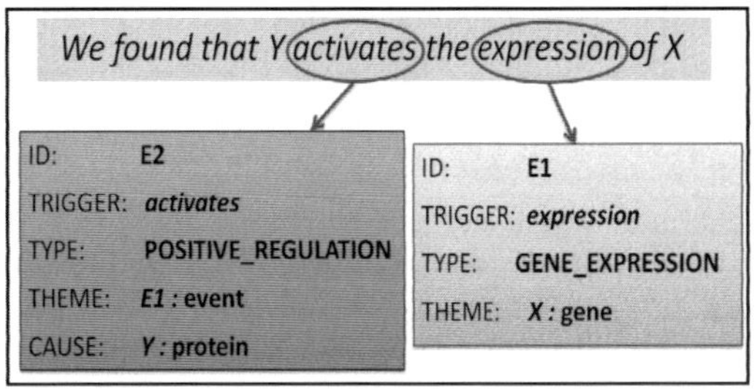

Figure 1. Bio-Event Representation

3.2 Meta-knowledge Annotation

Until recently, the only attempts to recognise information relating to the correct interpretation of events were restricted to sparse details regarding negation and speculation (Kim et al., 2011).

[1] http://www.sapientaproject.com/software
[2] http://uima.apache.org/

In order to address this problem, a multi-dimensional annotation scheme especially tailored to bio-events was developed (Nawaz et al., 2010; Thompson et al., 2011). The scheme identifies and categorises several different types of contextual details regarding events (termed *meta-knowledge*), including discourse information. Different types of meta-knowledge are encoded through five distinct dimensions (Figure 2). The advantage of using multiple dimensions is that the interplay between the assigned values in each dimension can reveal both subtle and substantial differences in the types of meta-knowledge expressed.

In the majority of cases, meta-knowledge is expressed through the presence of particular "clue" words or phrases, although other features can also come into play, such as the tense of the event trigger, or the relative position within the text.

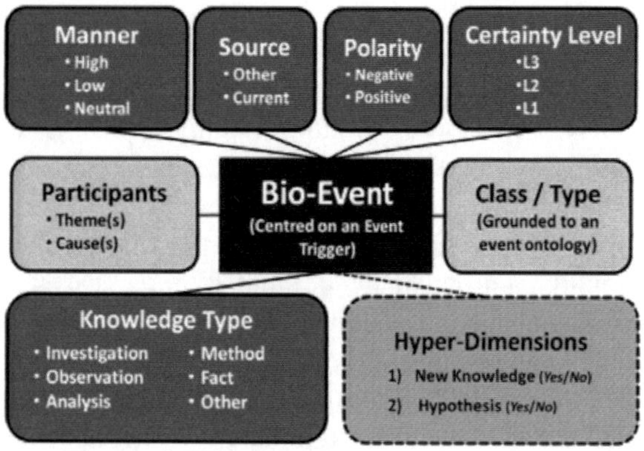

Figure 2: Meta-knowledge annotation

The annotation task consists of assigning an appropriate value from a fixed set for each dimension, as well as marking the textual evidence for this assignment. The five meta-knowledge dimensions and their values are as follows:

Knowledge Type (KT): Captures the general information content of the event. Each event is classified as one of: *Investigation* (enquiries and examinations, etc.), *Observation* (direct experimental observations), *Analysis* (inferences, interpretations and conjectures, etc.), *Fact* (known facts), *Method* (methods) or *Other* (general events that provide incomplete information or do not fit into any other category).

Certainty Level (CL): Encodes the confidence or certainty level ascribed to the event in the given text. The epistemic scale is partitioned into three distinct levels: *L3* (no expression of uncertainty), *L2* (high confidence or slight speculation) and *L1* (low confidence or considerable speculation).

Polarity: Identifies negated events. Negation is defined as the absence or non-existence of an entity or a process.

Manner: Captures information about the rate, level, strength or intensity of the event, using three values: *High*, *Low*, or *Neutral* (no indication of rate/intensity).

Source: Encodes the source of the knowledge being expressed by the event as *Current* (the current study) or *Other* (any other source).

Of these five dimensions, only *KT*, *CL* and *Source* were considered during the comparison with the other two schemes, since they are directly related to discourse analysis.

The GENIA event corpus, consisting of 1000 abstracts with 36,115 events (Kim et al., 2008) has been annotated with meta-knowledge by 2 annotators, supported by 64-page annotation guidelines [3] (Thompson et al., 2011). Inter-annotator agreement rates ranged between 0.84–0.93 (Cohen's Kappa). Research has been carried out into the automatic assignment of Manner values to events (Nawaz et al., In Press). In addition, the EventMine-MK service (Miwa et al., In Press), based on EventMine (Miwa et al., 2010) facilitates automatic extraction of biomedical events with meta-knowledge assigned. The performance of EventMine-MK in assigning different meta-knowledge values to events ranges between 57% and 87% (macro-averaged F-Score) on the BioNLP'09 Shared Task corpus (Kim et al, 2011). EventMine-MK is available as a component of the U-Compare interoperable text mining system[4] (Kano et al., 2011).

4 Clause annotation: Segments for epistemic knowledge

The third scheme we consider uses a Discourse Segment Type classification of segments at, roughly, a clause level, i.e., each segment has a main verb. This means that the level of granularity of argumentational elements in this scheme lies between the other two schemes, i.e. it is usually more granular than CoreSC, but sometimes less granular than the event-based scheme.

[3] http://www.nactem.ac.uk/meta-knowledge/
[4] http://www.nactem.ac.uk/ucompare/

Segment	Description	Examples
Fact	knowledge accepted to be true, a known fact.	*mature miR-373 is a homolog of miR-372,*
Hypothesis	a proposed idea, not supported by evidence	*This could for instance be a result of high mdm2 levels*
Problem	unresolved, contradictory, or unclear issue	*However, further investigation is required to demonstrate the exact mechanism of LATS2 action*
Goal	research goal	*To identify novel functions of miRNAs,*
Method	experimental method	*Using fluorescence microscopy and luciferase assays,*
Result	a restatement of the outcome of an experiment	*all constructs yielded high expression levels of mature miRNAs*
Implication	an interpretation of the results, in light of data	*our procedure is sensitive enough to detect mild growth differences*
Other-Hypothesis	an idea proposed by others	*[It is generally believed that] transcription factors are the final common pathway driving differentiation]*
Regulatory-Hypothesis	a matrix clause introducing a hypothesis	*It is generally believed that [transcription factors are the final common pathway driving differentiation]*

Table 2: Discourse Segment Types

The segment annotation scheme identifies a taxonomy of discourse segment types that seem to be exclusive and useful (de Waard & Pander Maat, 2009). Three classes of segment types are defined:

- Basic segment types: segments referring directly to the topic of study – see Table 2.
- 'Other'-segment types: segments referring to conceptual or experimental work in other research papers than the current one
- Regulatory segment types: 'regulatory' clauses that control and introduce other segments.

A list of segment types is presented in Table 2; further details, including a list of all segment types and correlations with verb tense can be found in de Waard & Pander Maat (2009). The focus of this work is to identify linguistic features that characterise these discourse segment types, according to three aspects:

- Verb tense, aspect, mood and voice
- Semantic verb class
- Epistemic modality markers

So far, 6 full-text papers (comprising about 2300 segments) have been manually annotated with segment types and correlated with the above features. A first automated validation was promising (de Waard, Buitelaar and Eigener, 2009). The need for parsing at a clause level is especially prominent in biological text, since specific semantic roles are played by particular clause types. We give four examples of typical clause constructions that play a specific rhetorical role: firstly, reporting clauses are often sentence-initial 'that' matrix clauses (1a):

1. a. This suggests that

1.b. miR-372 and miR-373 caused the observed selective growth advantage.

Secondly, descriptions confirming certain accepted characteristics of biological entities are often given as nonrestrictive relative clauses (2b):

2.a. We also generated BJ/ET cells expressing the RASV12-ERTAM chimera gene,

2. b. which is only active when tamoxifen is added

Thirdly, a subordinate gerund clause is often used to describe a method (3a), with a main (finite) clause describing a result (3b) and fourthly, experimental goals are often given as a (mostly sentence-initial) clause with a to-infinitive (4a) often preceding a past-tense methods clause (4b).

3. a. Using fluorescence microscopy and luciferase assays,

b. we observed potent and specific miRNA activity expressed from each miR-Vec (Figure S2).

4. a. To identify miRNAs that can interfere with this process

4. b. we transduced BJ/ET fibroblasts with miR-Lib

However, the lack of simple robust clause parsers has prevented the automated identification of semantic roles at the clause level. Therefore, this scheme has so far only been manually implemented. Despite being less widely implemented than the other two schemes, we believe that the segment scheme offers some useful pointers for linguistic features that can identify particular rhetorical classes in the text, and secondly, offers an interesting perspective on the fact that in biological text, several rhetorical moves are made within a single sentence.

5 Data and methods

Three papers already annotated according to the GENIA event annotation scheme (Kim et al., 2008), were further annotated according to the three annotation schemes described above. We obtained all corresponding CoreSCs, events and segments per sentence. Each sentence has a single CoreSC annotation and one or more segment annotations (depending on the number of clauses). Event annotations in a sentence may range from zero to multiple, according to whether any relevant biomedical events are described in the sentence.

Events within a sentence are mapped to segments by identifying which segment contains the trigger for a particular event. The three meta-knowledge dimensions for events considered in this comparison, i.e., KT, CL and Source, result in 16 different combinations of values encountered in the three papers. The numbers for CoreSC and Segment labels encountered were 12 and 22, respectively. Confusion matrices were obtained for each paper and for each pair of annotation schemes. Note that, as bio-events are largely unconcerned with describing methodology, the *Methods* sections of these papers do not contain event annotation or meta-knowledge annotation. The pairwise confusion matrices from each paper were combined, resulting in three matrices (Tables 3, 4 and 5), which describe the associations between the annotation schemes in the three papers examined. We have highlighted the highest frequencies per row and where appropriate also the highest values per column. The use of two different colours aims to facilitate readability.

6 Results and Discussion

We present the results from analysing the pairwise confusion matrices for the three schemes and discuss the merits of each scheme.

6.1 Event Meta-knowledge v. CoreSC

In Tables 3 (and 5), the meta-knowledge categories combine KT, CL and Source ((O)ther) values. Table 3 shows some straightforward and expected mappings, e.g.,Method (Met,L3) events are almost always found within CoreSC Experiment or Method sentences, whilst Investigation events (Inv,L3) occur most frequently within CoreSC Goal or Motivation sentences.

For other categories, information from the two schemes can complement each other in different ways. For example, KT and Source information about events can help to distinguish different types of information within CoreSC Background sentences (top left corner of Table 3). Such information mainly corresponds to facts, observations from previous studies, or analyses of information. Conversely, information from the CoreSC scheme can help to further classify the interpretation of events. For example, events with an analytical interpretation (Ana,L1,L2,L3) may occur as background information to a study (Bac), as hypotheses (Hyp), as part of observations (Obs), when reporting the results of the current study (Res) or when making concluding remarks about the study (Con). CoreSCs can also help to further refine events relating to outcomes (Obs,L3) according to whether they pertain to (Obs)ervations, (Res)ults or (Con)clusions.

CoreSC Conclusion, Result and Observation sentences contain mainly Observation events concerned with the current study. However, such sentences often also include an analytical part, with varying levels of certainty, which event information can help to isolate. The CL annotated for events is also useful in helping to determine the confidence with which information is stated in CoreSC Conclusion and Hypothesis sentences.

Due to the nature of bio-event annotation, only a small number of events correspond to methods. Thus, CoreSC provides a more detailed characterisation of method-related sentences, i.e., Experiment, Method_New, Model and Object.

6.2 Discourse Segments v. CoreSC

In most cases, there seems to be natural mapping between the two schemes (See Table 4). CoreSC Observation maps to *Result*, CoreSC Method and Experiment map to *Method*, CoreSC Hypothesis maps to *Hypothesis*, CoreSC Goal maps to *Goal*,

CoreSC Conclusion maps to *Implication* and *Hypothesis,* CoreSC Result maps to *Implication* and *Result*, and *Problem* is equivalent to CoreSC Motivation. The bulk of CoreSC Background maps to *Fact* and *Other-Implication*, but the "Other" Segment categories provide a substantial refinement of the CoreSC Background category.

	Bac	Con	Exp	Goa	Hyp	Met_New	Met_Old	Mod	Mot	Obj_New	Obs	Res
0	42	24	49	7	7	25	1	13	6	7	47	54
Obs,L3,O	166	0	0	0	0	0	3	0	12	0	0	2
Ana,L3,O	33	1	0	0	0	0	0	1	0	0	0	0
Ana,L2,O	3	0	0	0	0	0	0	0	0	0	0	0
Fact,L3,O	7	0	0	0	0	0	0	0	0	0	0	0
Fact,L3	24	1	0	1	0	0	0	0	5	3	0	2
Oth,L3	125	30	0	8	16	5	3	2	8	3	9	42
Ana,L1	2	10	0	0	6	0	0	0	1	0	0	6
Ana,L2	30	15	0	1	14	0	0	2	1	0	8	33
Ana,L3	11	11	0	0	2	1	2	0	3	0	14	28
Met,L3	4	1	15	1	0	5	0	0	0	0	2	6
Inv,L2	0	0	0	0	0	0	0	0	0	0	1	1
Inv,L3	5	3	1	6	2	4	3	0	8	0	1	1
Inv,L3,O	0	0	0	0	2	0	1	0	0	0	0	0
Obs,L1	1	0	0	0	0	0	0	0	0	0	0	0
Obs,L2	1	0	0	0	0	0	0	0	0	0	1	0
Obs,L3	31	34	3	1	10	3	0	2	7	1	59	87

Table 3. Event Meta-knowledge vs CoreSC

On the other hand, CoreSC refines *Method*, *Result* and *Implication* segments. CoreSC Result may include both *Fact* and *Method* clauses, which can be captured by the Segment scheme, since annotation is performed at the clause level. CoreSC Conclusion maps to both *Implication* and *Hypothesis* segments, suggesting that there may be differences in the certainty levels of these conclusions. This is supported by preliminary classification experiments (paper in progress).

6.3 Discourse Segments v. Event Meta-Knowledge

Some straightforward mappings exist between segment and event meta-knowledge categories (Table 5). For example, Investigation events (Inv, L3) are generally found within *Goal* and *Problem* segments; Method events (Met,L3) are normally found within *Method* segments, Observation events (Obs,L3) are found mainly within *Result*, *Fact* and *Implication* segments and (Ana,L1,L2) events correspond mainly to Hypotheses and Implications.

Whilst these are similar findings to the comparison between event meta-knowledge and CoreSCs, the variance of the distribution is often smaller when mapping from Events to Segments. This is to be expected – the information encoded by many events has the scope of roughly a clause, which corresponds closely to the scope of discourse segments. This could permit cleaner one-to-one mappings between categories.

	Bac	Con	Exp	Goa	Hyp	Met_New	Met_Old	Mod	Mot	Obj_New	Obs	Res
Fact	118	3	0	3	7	0	0	1	15	7	5	34
OtherFact	70	4	0	0	0	0	0	3	1	0	0	0
OtherGoal	2	1	0	0	0	0	0	0	0	0	0	0
OtherHypothesis	14	0	0	0	0	0	0	0	0	0	0	0
OtherImplication	124	1	0	0	3	0	0	1	5	0	0	1
OtherMethod	5	0	0	0	0	0	3	0	0	0	0	2
OtherProblem	1	0	0	0	0	0	0	0	0	0	0	0
OtherResult	64	1	0	0	0	0	6	0	0	3	0	9
RegFact	1	3	0	0	0	0	0	0	0	0	0	2
Implication	13	58	0	0	2	0	0	3	1	0	3	80
RegImplication	5	6	0	1	0	0	0	0	0	0	1	10
Method	6	2	54	2	2	32	0	6	1	0	8	13
Goal	2	0	5	12	6	9	2	2	4	0	0	5
RegGoal	0	1	0	0	0	0	0	0	0	0	0	0
Hypothesis	24	31	0	5	34	1	0	5	0	0	0	12
RegHypothesis	6	4	0	0	2	0	0	1	0	0	0	2
Problem	7	6	0	0	0	0	2	0	11	0	0	2
RegProblem	0	3	0	0	0	0	0	0	0	0	0	0
Result	13	6	1	1	2	0	0	2	8	0	112	75
RegResult	1	0	0	0	0	0	0	0	0	1	1	2
Intertextual	4	0	7	0	1	0	0	0	0	0	0	3
Intratextual	2	0	1	0	0	0	0	2	0	0	8	4

Table 4: Segments vs CoreSC

Hypothesis and *Implication* segments mainly contain (Ana)lysis events. The differing certainty levels of events can help to refine information about the statements made within these segments. Likewise, these segment types could help to refine the nature of the analysis described by the event.

Similarly to the CoreSC scheme, the results suggest that *Result* segments could be refined by the meta-knowledge scheme to distinguish between results emerging from direct experimental observations, and those obtained through analysis of experimental observations. Another interesting result is that *Fact* segments can contain Fact, (Ana)lysis or (Obs)ervation events. This may suggest that *Fact* segments are actually a rather general category, containing a range of different information. Few events occur within the *Regulatory* segments, as these mainly introduce content-bearing segments.

The majority of *Method* segments and a significant number of the *Result* segments do not correspond to events, as none of the methods sections have been annotated with event information, for reasons explained previously.

	0	Ana	Ana	Ana	Ana	Ana	Fact	Fact	Met	Oth	Inv	Inv	Inv	Obs	Obs	Obs	Obs
		L1	L2	L2,O	L3	L3,O	L3	L3,O	L3	L3	L2	L3	L3,O	L1	L2	L3	L3,O
Hypothesis	8	18	26	1	0	0	0	0	1	39	0	4	1	0	0	14	0
Implication	22	2	30	0	34	2	2	0	0	38	2	1	0	0	0	27	0
OtherHypothesis	0	0	3	1	0	0	0	0	0	9	0	1	0	0	0	0	0
OtherImplication	8	1	6	1	4	28	0	3	3	27	0	2	0	1	0	5	46
RegImplication	11	0	2	0	0	1	0	0	0	5	0	1	0	0	0	3	0
RegHypothesis	1	0	0	0	0	0	0	0	0	6	0	1	0	0	0	7	0
Fact	15	0	18	0	6	0	28	0	0	55	0	1	0	0	1	44	25
RegFact	0	0	0	0	0	0	0	0	0	1	0	0	0	0	0	5	0
OtherGoal	1	0	0	0	0	0	0	0	0	2	0	0	0	0	0	0	0
OtherProblem	0	0	0	0	0	0	0	0	0	1	0	0	0	0	0	0	0
Method	80	0	1	0	0	0	0	0	23	9	0	2	0	0	0	8	3
OtherMethod	7	0	0	0	0	0	0	0	0	0	0	2	1	0	0	0	0
Goal	13	0	0	0	0	0	1	0	0	18	0	11	1	0	0	3	0
RegGoal	1	0	0	0	0	0	0	0	0	0	0	0	0	0	0	0	0
Problem	9	4	0	0	2	0	0	0	0	5	0	8	0	0	0	0	0
RegProblem	3	0	0	0	0	0	0	0	0	0	0	0	0	0	0	0	0
Result	51	0	14	0	20	0	0	0	6	18	0	0	0	0	1	103	7
OtherResult	11	0	1	0	0	1	0	1	0	10	0	0	0	0	0	12	47
OtherFact	4	0	1	0	0	2	5	3	0	7	0	0	0	0	0	2	54
RegResult	5	0	0	0	0	0	0	0	0	0	0	0	0	0	0	0	0
Intertextual	13	0	0	0	0	0	0	0	0	1	0	0	0	0	0	1	0
Intratextual	17	0	0	0	0	0	0	0	0	0	0	0	0	0	0	0	0

Table 5: Segments vs Event Meta-Knowledge

7 Related Work

A number of schemes for annotating scientific discourse elements at the sentence level have been proposed. Certain schemes have been aimed at abstracts, e.g., (McKnight & Srinivasan, 2003; Ruch et al., 2007; Hirohata et al., 2008; Björne et al., 2009). The work of Hirohata et al. (2009) has been integrated with the MEDIE service[5] (Miyao et al., 2006), allowing the user to query facts using conclusions, results, etc. For full papers, the most notable work has focussed on argumentative zoning (AZ) (Teufel et al., 1999; Teufel & Moens, 2002; Teufel et al., 2009; Teufel, 2010). An important aspect of AZ involves capturing the attribution of knowledge claims and citation function, and the scheme has been tested on information extraction and summarisation tasks with Computational Linguistics papers. AZ was modified for the annotation of biology papers by Mizuta et al. (2005) in order to facilitate information extraction, and more recently Teufel et al. (2009) extended the AZ scheme to better accommodate the life sciences and chemistry in particular, producing AZ-II.

Scientific discourse annotation has also targeted the retrieval of *speculative text* to help improve curation. For a recent overview see de Waard and Pander Maat (2012). Modality and negation in text have also been the focus of recent workshops (Farkas et al (2010), Morante & Sporleder (2012)). Finally, Shatkay et al (2008) define a multi-dimensional scheme, which combines several of the above-mentioned aspects.

Recent work has compared schemes to discover mappings and relative merits. Liakata et al. (2010) compared AZ-II and CoreSC on 36 papers annotated with both schemes and found that CoreSC provides finer granularity in distinguishing content categories (e.g. methods, goals and outcomes) while the strength of AZ-II lies in detecting the attribution of knowledge claims and identifying the different functions of background information. Guo et al. (2010) compared three schemes for the identification of discourse structure in scientific abstracts from cancer research assessment articles. The work showed a subsumption relation between the scheme of Hirohata et al. (2008), a cut-down version of the scheme proposed by Teufel et al. (2009) and CoreSC (1st layer), from general to specific.

8 Conclusion

We have compared three different schemes, each taking a different perspective to the annotation of scientific discourse. The comparison shows that the three schemes are complementary, with different strengths and points of focus. CoreSC offers a fine-grained characterisation of methods, outcomes and objectives. It has been used to annotate a collection of 265 full papers, and subsequently CoreSC recognition has been fully automated, creating the online SAPIENTA tool. The discourse segment annotation scheme can help to provide a finer-grained characterisation of background work, and could also help to split multi-clause CoreSC sentences into appropriate segments. Recognition of event meta-knowledge has been fully automated in the U-Compare framework, and the KT values of the scheme can help to provide a finer-grained analysis of certain segment and sentence types. The CL dimension also allows confidence values to be ascribed to the Conclusion, Result, Implication and Hypothesis categories of the other two schemes.

Future work will focus on annotating texts with several discourse perspectives to investigate the advantages of the schemes. Ideally we would like to propose a unified approach for scientific discourse annotation, but recognize that choices such as the unit of annotation are often task-oriented, and that users should be able to mix and match discourse segments as required. This said, the analysis in this paper paves the way for potential harmonisation, revealing points of union and intersection between the schemes.

Acknowledgements

This work has been supported through funding for Maria Liakata by JISC, the Leverhulme Trust and EBI-EMBL. It has also been supported by the BBSRC through grant number BB/G013160/1UK (Automated Biological Event Extraction from the Literature for Drug Discovery), the MetaNet4U project (ICT PSP Programme, Grant Agreement: No. 270893) and the JISC-funded ISHER project.

[5] http://www.nactem.ac.uk/medie/

References

Ananiadou, S., Kell, D.B. and Tsujii, J. (2006). Text mining and its potential applications in systems biology. *Trends Biotechnol*, 24(12): 571-9.

Ananiadou, S. and McNaught, J., Eds. (2006). *Text Mining for Biology and Biomedicine*. Boston / London, Artech House.

Ananiadou, S., Pyysalo, S., Tsujii, J. and Kell, D.B. (2010). Event extraction for systems biology by text mining the literature. *Trends Biotechnol*, 28(7): 381-90.

Björne, J., Heimonen, J., Ginter, F., Airola, A., Pahikkala, T. and Salakoski, T. (2009). Extracting Complex Biological Events with Rich Graph-Based Feature Sets. In *Proceedings of the BioNLP 2009 Workshop Companion Volume for Shared Task*, pp. 10-18.

Blake, C. (2010). Beyond genes, proteins, and abstracts: Identifying scientific claims from full-text biomedical articles. *Journal of Biomedical Informatics*, 43(2): 173-189.

Cohen, J. (1960). A coefficient of agreement for nominal scales. *Educational and psychological measurement*, 20: 37-46.

Cohen, K.B. and Hunter, L. (2008). Getting started in text mining. *PLoS Comput Biol*, 4(1): e20.

Cohen, K.B., Johnson, H.L., Verspoor, K., Roeder, C. and Hunter, L.E. (2010). The structural and content aspects of abstracts versus bodies of full text journal articles are different. *BMC Bioinformatics*, 11: 492.

de Waard, A., Buitelaar, P., Eigner, T. (2009). *Identifying the epistemic value of discourse segments in biology texts*. Proceedings of the Eighth International Conference on Computational Semantics, pp. 351-354

de Waard, A. and Pander Maat, H. (2009). Categorizing Epistemic Segment Types in Biology Research Articles. In *Proceedings of the Workshop on Linguistic and Psycholinguistic Approaches to Text Structuring (LPTS 2009)*

de Waard, A. and Pander Maat, H. (2012). Knowledge Attribution in Scientific Discourse: A Taxonomy of Types and Overview of Features, In *Proceedings of the Workshop on Detecting Structure in Scholarly Discourse (DSDD)*, ACL 2012.

Farkas, R. Vincze, V., Móra, G., Csirik, J. and Szarvas, G. 2010. The CoNLL-2010 Shared Task: Learning to Detect Hedges and their Scope in Natural Language Text. In *Proceedings of the Fourteenth Conference on Computational Natural Language Learning*, Uppsala, Sweden. Association for Computational Linguistics, pp. 1- 12.

Guo, Y., Korhonen, A., Liakata, M., Silins, I., LiSun, L. and Stenius, U. (2010). Identifying the information structure of scientific abstracts: An investigation of three different schemes. In *Proceedings of BioNLP 2010*, pp. 99-107.

Hirohata, K., Okazaki, N., Ananiadou, S. and Ishizuka, M. (2008). Identifying Sections in Scientific Abstracts using Conditional Random Fields. In *Proceedings of the 3rd International Joint Conference on Natural Language Processing*, pp. 381-388.

Hyland, K. (1996). Writing without conviction? Hedging in science research articles. *Applied Linguistics*, 17(4): 433-454.

Kano, Y., Miwa, M., Cohen, K.B., Hunter, L.E., Ananiadou, S. and Tsujii, J. (2011). U-Compare: A modular NLP workflow construction and evaluation system. *IBM Journal of Research and Development*, 55(3): 11:1-11:10.

Kilicoglu, H. and Bergler, S. (2008). Recognizing speculative language in biomedical research articles: a linguistically motivated perspective. *BMC Bioinformatics*, 9(Suppl 11): S10.

Kim, J.-D., Ohta, T. and Tsujii, J. (2008). Corpus annotation for mining biomedical events from literature. *BMC Bioinformatics*, 9(10).

Kim, J.D., Ohta, T., Pyysalo, S., Kano, Y. and Tsujii, J. (2011). Extracting Bio-Molecular Events from Literature - The BioNLP'09 Shared Task. *Computational Intelligence*, 27(4): 513-540.

Liakata, M., Saha, S., Dobnik, S., Batchelor, C. and Rebholz-Schuhmann, D. (2012). Automatic recognition of conceptualisation zones in scientific articles and two life science applications. *Bioinformatics*, 28 (7).

Liakata, M. and Soldatova, L.N. (2009). The ART corpus. Technical Report. Aberystwth University.

Liakata, M., Teufel, S., Siddharthan, A. and Batchelor, C. (2010). Corpora for the conceptualisation and zoning of scientific papers. In *Proceedings of LREC*, pp. 2054-2061.

Light, M., Qiu, X.Y. and Srinivasan, P. (2004). The language of bioscience: Facts, speculations, and statements in between. In *Proceedings of the BioLink 2004 Workshop at HLT/NAACL*, pp. 17–24.

McKnight, L. and Srinivasan, P. (2003). Categorization of sentence types in medical abstracts. In *AMIA Annu Symp Proc*, pp. 440-4.

Miwa, M., Saetre, R., Kim, J.D. and Tsujii, J. (2010). Event extraction with complex event classification using rich features. *J Bioinform Comput Biol*, 8(1): 131-46.

Miwa, M., Thompson, P. and Ananiadou, S. (2012). Boosting automatic event extraction from the literature using domain adaptation and coreference resolution. *Bioinformatics.*

Miwa, M., Thompson, P., McNaught, J, Kell, D.B and Ananiadou, S. (In Press). Extracting semantically enriched events from biomedical literature. *BMC Bioinformatics.*

Miyao, Y., Ohta, T., Masuda, K., Tsuruoka, Y., Yoshida, K., Ninomiya, T. and Tsujii, J. (2006). Semantic Retrieval for the Accurate Identification of Relational Concepts in Massive Textbases. In *Proceedings of ACL*, pp. 1017-1024.

Mizuta, Y., Korhonen, A., Mullen, T. and Collier, N. (2005). Zone Analysis in Biology Articles as a Basis for Information Extraction. *International Journal of Medical Informatics*,75(6): 468-487.

Morante R., and Sporleder C, (2012). Modality and negation: An introduction to the special issue. *Computational Linguistics,* 38(2): 1–38.

Nawaz, R., Thompson, P. and Ananiadou, S. (In Press). Identification of Manner in Bio-Events. *Proceedings of the Eighth International Conference on Language Resources and Evaluation (LREC 2012).*

Nawaz, R., Thompson, P., McNaught, J. and Ananiadou, S. (2010). Meta-Knowledge Annotation of Bio-Events. In *Proceedings of LREC 2010*, pp. 2498-2507.

Pyysalo, S., Ginter, F., Heimonen, J., Bjorne, J., Boberg, J., Jarvinen, J. and Salakoski, T. (2007). BioInfer: a corpus for information extraction in the biomedical domain. *BMC Bioinformatics*, 8: 50.

Pyysalo, S., Ohta, T., Rak, R., Sullivan, D., Mao, C., Wang, C., Sobral, B., Tsujii, J. and Ananiadou, S. (In Press). Overview of the ID, EPI and REL tasks of BioNLP Shared Task 2011. *BMC Bioinformatics.*

Quirk, C., Choudhury, P., Gamon, M. and Vanderwende, L. (2011). MSR-NLP Entry in BioNLP Shared Task 2011. In *Proceedings of BioNLP Shared Task 2011 Workshop*, pp. 155-163.

Ruch, P., Boyer, C., Chichester, C., Tbahriti, I., Geissbuhler, A., Fabry, P., Gobeill, J., Pillet, V., Rebholz-Schuhmann, D., Lovis, C. and Veuthey, A.L. (2007). Using argumentation to extract key sentences from biomedical abstracts. *Int J Med Inform*, 76(2-3): 195-200.

Sándor, Á. (2007). Modeling metadiscourse conveying the author's rhetorical strategy in biomedical research abstracts. *Revue Française de Linguistique Appliquée*, 200(2): 97-109.

Shatkay, H., Pan, F., Rzhetsky, A. and Wilbur, W.J. (2008). Multi-dimensional classification of biomedical text: toward automated, practical provision of high-utility text to diverse users. *Bioinformatics*, 24(18): 2086-2093.

Soldatova, L.N. and King, R.D. (2006). An ontology of scientific experiments. *Journal of the Royal Society Interface*, 3(11): 795-803.

Soldatova, L.N. and Liakata, M. (2007). An ontology methodology and cisp-the proposed core information about scientific papers., Aberystwyth University. Technical Report JISC Project Report.

Teufel, S. (2010). *The Structure of Scientific Articles: Applications to Citation Indexing and Summarization.* Stanford, CA, CSLI Publications.

Teufel, S., Carletta, J. and Moens, M. (1999). An annotation scheme for discourse-level argumentation in research articles. In *Proceedings of EACL*, pp. 110-117.

Teufel, S. and Moens, M. (2002). Summarizing scientific articles: experiments with relevance and rhetorical status. *Computational Linguistics*, 28(4): 409-445.

Teufel, S., Siddharthan, A. and Batchelor, C. (2009). Towards discipline-independent argumentative zoning: Evidence from chemistry and computational linguistics. In *Proceedings of EMNLP 2009*, pp. 1493-1502.

Thompson, P., Iqbal, S.A., McNaught, J. and Ananiadou, S. (2009). Construction of an annotated corpus to support biomedical information extraction. *BMC Bioinformatics*, 10: 349.

Thompson, P., Nawaz, R., McNaught, J. and Ananiadou, S. (2011). Enriching a biomedical event corpus with meta-knowledge annotation. *BMC Bioinformatics*, 12: 393.

Vincze, V., Szarvas, G., Farkas, R., Mora, G. and Csirik, J. (2008). The BioScope corpus: biomedical texts annotated for uncertainty, negation and their scopes. *BMC Bioinformatics*, 9(Suppl 11): S9.

Zweigenbaum, P., Demner-Fushman, D., Yu, H. and Cohen, K.B. (2007). Frontiers of biomedical text mining: current progress. *Briefings in Bioinformatics*, 8(5): 358-375.

Epistemic Modality and Knowledge Attribution in Scientific Discourse: A Taxonomy of Types and Overview of Features

Anita de Waard
Elsevier Labs
Jericho, VT, USA
a.dewaard@elsevier.com

Henk Pander Maat
Utrecht Institute of Linguistics
Utrecht, The Netherlands
h.l.w.pandermaat@uu.nl

Abstract

We propose a model for knowledge attribution and epistemic evaluation in scientific discourse, consisting of three dimensions with different values: source (author, other, unknown); value (unknown, possible, probable, presumed true) and basis (reasoning, data, other). Based on a literature review, we investigate four linguistic features that mark different types epistemic evaluation (modal auxiliary verbs, adverbs/adjectives, reporting verbs and references). A corpus study on two biology papers indicates the usefulness of this model, and suggest some typical trends. In particular, we find that matrix clauses with a reporting verb of the form '*These results suggest*', are the predominant feature indicating knowledge attribution in scientific text.

1 Introduction

Our main research goal is to linguistically "specify the precise time and place in the process of fact construction when a statement became transformed into a fact", as Latour and Woolgar (1979) put it. Specifically, we are interested in creating a linguistically motivated framework of biological sensemaking to help extract newly claimed knowledge from large text corpora.

Biological understanding consists of a conceptual model of the system at study, which is collaboratively created by the scientists working on that system. In contributing a new building block to the model, authors will need to argue, first: that their experiments are appropriate, and performed well; second, that they can draw certain conclusions from these experiments; and third, that, and how, these conclusions fit within the existing knowledge model for their field. Their observations and inferences might confirm or contradict other thoughts about the model, expressed in other papers. This need to indicate certainty and agreement/disagreement means that biological papers contain many explicit truth evaluations of their own and other authors' propositions (epistemic modality), and where needed, the explicit attribution of the creator of the propositions (knowledge attribution[1]). Therefore, to understand how biological knowledge is formulated in language, it is essential to understand the linguistic mechanisms of modality and attribution.

In this paper, we present an overview of work in linguistics, genre studies, bioinformatics and computational linguistics, related to epistemic evaluation. From this, we distill a three-tiered taxonomy and a set of linguistic cues or markers that distinguish various forms of epistemic evaluation. We try out this taxonomy and marker set in a small manual corpus exploration of two biology papers, and discuss some correlations between different types and market. We conclude with a proposal for the application of this work.

2 Epistemic Evaluation Taxonomy

2.1 Overview of current work

Strictly speaking, every factual proposition or piece of Propositional Content (Hengeveld and Mackenzie, 2008) contains an (implicit) epistemic evaluation: if a statement is given without further comment on its truth value, we read – irony aside – that the author agrees with the proposition it contains. '*Water is wet.*' – or '*LPS-induced IL-6*

[1] To avoid the use of the cumbersome contraction 'epistemic modality evaluation and knowledge attribution' we will henceforth use the term 'epistemic evaluation' to cover both evaluation and attribution.

gene transcription in murine monocytes is controlled by NF-B' are statements that do not contain any epistemic modifiers, and are therefore read to be unconditionally accepted by the author. In other cases, however, this truth value is modified: '*These results suggest that water is wet.*' or attributed: '*Author X et al. (2010) report that water is wet.*' Here, we investigate modifiers of propositional content that define either epistemic modality, i.e. the degree of authorial commitment to a proposition, e.g. '*5' untranslated exon 1 may have a regulatory function*', or knowledge attribution: the source of the propositional knowledge, such as when a reference indicates the source of the claim: '*GATA-1 transactivates the EOS47 promoter through a site in the 5'UTR [34].*' There is a body of work pertaining to knowledge attribution and epistemic evaluation in scientific text, within at least four different fields: linguistics, genre studies, bioinformatics, and sentiment detection. A detailed overview of the hedging types and markers found in this literature overview is posted in Dataverse (de Waard, 2012) but we will provide a summary here.

Within linguistics, truth evaluations and source attributions are an important subject within most modern theories of language; here, only a small overview of some pertinent theories can be given. Hengeveld and Mackenzie (2008) characterize truth evaluations as 'modifiers of Propositional Content', concerning 'the kind and degree of commitment of a rational being to Propositional Content, or a specification of the (non-verbal) source of the Propositional Content'. These two categories – knowledge evaluation and knowledge attribution- are also indicated by the concepts 'epistemic modality' and 'evidentiality', respectively. De Haan (1999) strongly argues that they are separate phenomena – and we agree – but for our purposes, establishing modes of truth evaluation and attribution in scientific text, both are relevant. Verstraete (2001) distinguishes between objective and subjective modality: in an objectively modal clause, the truth value of the state of knowledge is brought into question ('*This subject is unknown*'), but the certainty the author has pertaining to the clause is not; in a subjective modal clause, the author expresses uncertainty regarding the extent of his or her knowledge ('*It might be (that this is the case)*').

In genre studies, a body of work revolves around the concept of *hedging*: 'the expression of tentativeness and possibility in language' (Lakoff, 1972; Hyland, 1995). The focus here is on the rhetorical/sociological motivation for, and surface features of, these 'politeness markers'. Myers (1992) identifies stereotypical sentence patterns for hedging from a corpus study of fifty related articles in molecular genetics. Salager-Meyer (1994) defines hedging as presenting 'the true state of the writers' understanding, namely, the strongest claim a careful researcher can make.' She identifies three reasons for hedging: (1) that of purposive fuzziness and vagueness (threat- minimizing strategy); (2) that which reflects the authors' modesty for their achievements and avoidance of personal involvement; and (3) that related to the impossibility or unwillingness of reaching absolute accuracy and of quantifying all the phenomena under observation. Very influentially, Hyland (1995, 2005) proposes an explanatory framework for scientific hedging which combines sociological, linguistic, and discourse analytic perspectives and proposes a three-part taxonomy, distinguishing writer-oriented, accuracy-oriented and reader-oriented hedges. Countering Hyland, Crompton (1997) reviews and evaluates some of the different ways in which the term 'hedge' has been defined in the literature thus far. His new definition is that 'a hedge is an item of language, which a speaker uses to explicitly qualify his/her lack of commitment to the truth of a proposition he/she utters.' Martín-Martín (2008) analyses three different hedging strategies and multiple surface features for hedging in a corpus of full-text papers in English and Spanish, and presents a detailed taxonomy of hedging types and cues, based on literature and corpus studies.

Within bioinformatics and bio-computational linguistics, a body of work has been done on identifying 'speculative language' (Light, 2004). The main purpose here is to enable the automated identification of truth and speculation, in order to enable the construction of databases of known, and candidate, biological facts. The differences with earlier discussions are twofold: first, there is less (or no) effort to study communicative functions: for instance, there is no interest in identifying the authors' rhetorical intent, or the sociological or political motivations for using a particular type of hedge. Second, bioinformatics focuses more on identifying different types of speculation: is the opinion presented positive or negative, strong or weak, etc. Light et al. (2004) annotate a corpus of Medline sentences as highly speculative, low speculative, or definite, and then train a classifier to automatically recognize speculative sentences. (As an interesting result, they find that almost all speculations appear in the final or penultimate sentence of the abstract).

Wilbur et al. (2006) are motivated by the need to identify and characterize locations in published papers where reliable scientific facts can be found, and present a set of guidelines and the results of an annotation task to annotate a full-text corpus with a five-dimensional set of quantities focus, polarity, certainty, evidence, and directionality. Of these, certainty and evidence relate to knowledge attribution and epistemic evaluation. Medlock and Briscoe (2007) develop a set of guidelines for identifying speculative sentences and an annotated corpus, to test their automated speculation classification tool. Kilicoglu and Bergler (2008) explore a linguistically motivated approach to the problem of recognizing speculative language in biomedical research articles. Building on Hyland's work, they identify **a set of syntactic patterns, which they use for detecting speculative sentences out of a corpus. Thompson et al. (2008) propose a multi-dimensional classification of** a preliminary set of words and phrases that express modality within biomedical texts, and present the results of an annotation experiment where sentences are annotated with level of speculation, type/source of the evidence and the level of certainty towards the statement writer or other. Vincze et al. (2008) describe the BioScope corpus, a collection of Medline abstracts and four full-text papers annotated with instances of negation and speculation.

In the subfield of computational linguistics pertaining to sentiment detection, the goal has been to create overviews of large set of documents summarizing collective opinions and emotion about some topic. Here a more 'mathematical' definition of modality is evolving, which considers the proposition being evaluated as being 'operated on' by the evaluator. A distinction is made between the holder of the opinion, and the strength, polarity and other attributes of the opinion. Similar to work in (bio)computational linguistics, this work has focused is on different types of opinions , and the clues that allow automated detection. Most work in this field has focused on other domains, such as news and product reviews, see e.g. Wilson and Wiebe (2003), Kim and Hovy (2004), and Tang et al., (2009).

2.2 Our proposal

Following the formalism used in opinion/sentiment analysis (e.g., Wilson and Wiebe, 2003; Hovy, 2011) and Functional Discourse Grammar (Hengeveld and Mackenzie, 2008) we differentiate between, firstly, Propositions (similar to FDG's Propositional Content), which can consist of either experimental (*'all thymocytes stained positive for GFP'*) or conceptual (*'CCR3 is expressed strongly on eosinophils'*) statements about the (conceived or acted upon/perceived) world, and secondly, modifiers, that modify on these Propositions and modify their truth value or the knowledge attribution. Building on the literature as summarized above, we define a taxonomy of epistemic evaluation along three facets:

1. Epistemic valuations possess a value or level of certainty. Both Hengeveld and Mackenzie (2008) and Wilbur et al. (2006) propose a tripartite division:
   - 'Doxastic' (firm belief in truth, Wilbur's category 3)
   - 'Dubitative' (some doubt about the truth exists; Wilbur's category 2)
   - 'Hypothetical' (where the truth value is only proposed; Wilbur's category 1)
   - Wilbur also adds the useful category 'Lack of knowledge' (level 0).

2. There can different bases of the evaluation:
   - Reasoning: based mostly or solely on argumentation, and not directly on data (e.g., *'it is thought that'*, *'we expected'*)
   - Data: based explicitly on data (e.g., *'these data suggest that'*, *'CCR3 has been shown to be'*)
   - Implicit or absent: if it is unclear what the evaluation or attribution is based on (e.g., *'GATA-1 transactivates the EOS47 promoter, through a site in the 5'UTR'*)

3. The source of the knowledge is identified:
   - Explicit source of knowledge: the knowledge evaluation can be explicitly

owned by the author ('*We therefore conclude that...*') or by a named referent ('*Vijh et al. [28] demonstrated that...*')
- Implicit source of knowledge: if there is no explicit source named, knowledge can implicitly still be attributed to the author ('*these results suggest...*') or an external source ('*It is generally believed that...*')
- No source of knowledge: the source of knowledge can be absent entirely, e.g. in factual statements, such as '*transcription factors are the final common pathway driving differentiation*'.

Table 1 summarizes our proposed classification.

3 Epistemic evaluation markers

To use our taxonomy to find instances and classes of epistemic evaluation in text, we need to know with what lexicogrammatical cues they are typically marked. Table A1 in the Appendix shows the details, but in summary, a literature review shows widespread agreement on the following cue types:

- Modal auxiliary verbs (e.g. *can, could, might*)
- Qualifying adverbs and adjectives (e.g. *interestingly, possibly, likely, potential, somewhat, slightly, powerful, unknown, undefined*)
- References, either external (e.g. '*[Voorhoeve et al., 2006]*') or internal (e.g. '*See fig. 2a*').
- Reporting verbs (e.g. *suggest, imply, indicate, show, seem* - see. e.g. Thomas and Hawes (1994) and Hyland (2005) for examples and definitions)

We decided not to add two further categories of epistemic evaluation cues that are often mentioned:

Personal pronouns. ('*we*', '*our results*', or similar). Closer analysis of the papers that mention this shows that in all cases where personal pronouns are mentioned as a hedging device, epistemic verbs are present, in phrases such as: '*we show*', '*our results suggest*', etc. Therefore, simply mentioning personal pronouns does not add a useful feature; it does lead to a great deal of false positives, since (first-)personal pronouns are often used in describing methods ('*next, we injected*', etc.)

Concept	Values
Value	0 - Lack of knowledge
	1 – Hypothetical: low certainty
	2 – Dubitative: higher likelihood but short of complete certainty
	3 – Doxastic: complete certainty, reflecting an accepted, known and/or proven fact.
Basis	R – Reasoning (*'Therefore, one can argue...'*)
	D – Data (*'These results suggest...'*)
	0 – Unidentified (*'Studies report that...'*)
Source	A - Author: Explicit mention of author/speaker or current paper as source (*'We hypothesize that...'; 'Figure 2a shows that...'*)
	N - Named external source, either explicitly or as a reference ('*...several reports have documented this expression [11-16,42].*')
	IA - Implicit attribution to the author ('*Electrophoretic mobility shift analysis revealed that...*')
	NN – Nameless external source ('*no eosinophil-specific transcription factors have been reported...*')
	0 – No source of knowledge ('*transcription factors are the final common pathway driving differentiation*')

Table 1: Proposed classification for epistemic modality and knowledge attribution

In a similar vein, passives are sometimes suggested as an indication of epistemic evaluation, but since they are e.g. often used in Methods sections ('*the rats were injected...*') they do not indicate markers of epistemic modality or attribution.

4 Small Test of Correlation between Epistemic Types and Cues

Using these four features, we want to explore whether all cases where epistemic evaluation occurs are covered by these cues; conversely, do the unmarked cases not have any cues? In other words, are the cues any good at identifying epistemic evaluation, and do certain clues identify certain types?

To investigate these issues, we conducted a small corpus study on two full-text papers in biology (Voorhoeve et. al, 2006; Zimmermann et al., 2005). First, we manually parsed them into clauses via the criteria outlined in (de Waard and

Pander Maat, 2009), leading to a total of 812 clauses. For each clause, we identified the epistemic/knowledge attribution value/source/basis according to the taxonomy in Table 1. Next, we identified the incidence of the four cue types under investigation: modal auxiliary verbs, qualifying adverbs/adjectives, reporting verbs (clauses containing a reporting verb and subordinate clauses controlled by matrix clause with a reporting verb), and references. A sample of this markup, with the clause, attribution/evaluation type, and presence or absence of markers, is given in Table A1.

This sample is too small to draw any quantitative conclusions from. However, we do believe our results support the validity of our model, in two ways: first, because we easily can identify a modality type (value/source/basis) for each of the 812 clauses, and second, because all statements of value < 3 are indicated by one of the four cue types which we have identified.

Next to these general findings, a few correlations between cue type and epistemic evaluation type become apparent (for details, see Table A2):

- Modal auxiliary verbs ('*might, can, could*') mark potentiality; in our sample, they only indicate clauses of 'possible' value (=1).
- Lack of cues indicates certainty. 47 out of 144 segments with value = 3 have no epistemic cues and no segments of value < 3 have no cues.
- Validating adverbs and adjectives rarely occur; when they do, they usually refer to 'Certain' segments (value = 3). These indicate focus and aim to draw attention to a finding or statement, and are: *important(ly)* (5x), *interestingly*, *striking* (*example*), *presumably*, and *apparently*.
- References mostly occur in 'Certain' segments. This can be because references usually occur when results are cited (3/D/N) or when reference to a figure is made (3/D/IA).
- Within our corpus, 44 discourse segments could not be classified as containing any type of knowledge attribution or evaluation. These were mostly goal statements ('*To identify this process…*') or methods reports ('*We injected all animals…*'). 16 of these (36%) did have a reporting verb (the reporting verbs used here were *analyze, address, assess, define, determine, identify, investigate*, *localize,* and *test*). 12 of these cases were indeed goal clauses containing a to-infinitive verb form.

These results suggest that a combination of verb tense/aspect as well as semantic verb class should be taken into account when analyzing cues for epistemic modality.

The one epistemic type that remains unidentified is 'lack of knowledge' (indicated by a knowledge value of 0); these are marked by different verb types, not just reporting verbs. These clauses are usually marked by specific negational forms of adverbs, verb forms, or nouns ('*has not been established*', '*is unknown*', '*yet to be determined*' etc. – see Table 2). Therefore, our markers do not adequately cover the 'lack of knowledge' case and finding these constructions by string matching is probably the best way to automate the identification of open research questions in text.

Overall, however, the most prevalent cue we observe is that of a reporting verb, either directly within a clause or governing it, in a matrix clause construction. Half of all statements with Value = 3, 90% of the statements with Value = 2 and 33% of the statements with Value = 1 either contain or are governed by (i.e. are a subordinate clause to a matrix clause containing) a reporting verb. Since this is such a strongly prevalent marker, we wanted to explore if certain reporting verbs perhaps specifically contribute to a particular type of modality.

In Table 2, we show the reporting verbs vs. the knowledge value found in the 812 clauses that we analyzed. Specifically, particular knowledge values can be associated with certain verbs:

- hypothetical statements are reported with '*hypothesize*' (5 x) and cognitive verbs such as '*think*' and '*suspect*', though they are also often indicated by a modal auxiliary, as discussed above;
- probable statements are marked by '*indicate*' (12x) and '*suggest*' (18 x);
- statements presumed to be true are indicated by '*find*' and especially '*demonstrate*' (15 x).

Value = 0 (Lack of Knowledge)	establish, (remain to be) elucidated, be (clear/useful), (remain to be) examined/determined, describe, make difficult to infer, report
Value = 1 (Hypothetical)	be important, consider, expect, hypothesize (5x), give insight, raise possibility that, suspect, think
Value = 2 (Dubitative)	appear, believe, implicate (2x), imply, indicate (12x), play a role, represent, suggest (18x), validate (2x)
Value = 3 (Doxastic)	be able/apparent/important /positive/visible, compare (2x), confirm (2x), define, demonstrate (15x), detect (5x), discover, display (3x), eliminate, find (3x), identify (4x), know, need, note (2x), observe (2x), obtain (success/results- 3x), prove to be, refer, report(2x), reveal (3x), see(2x) show (24x), study, view

Table 2: Reporting verbs vs. knowledge value for 2 papers

Since the segments containing these reporting verbs are so pivotal to knowledge attribution, they bear closer scrutiny. Generally these are sentence-initial clauses that adhere to the following word order (where Noun Phrases and Verb Phrases are always present, and the others are optional):

Adverb/Connective + Determiner + Adverb/Adjective + **NP** + Modal + Adjective + **VP** + Preposition

All values found in the 42 clauses of this type in one of the papers we examined (Zimmermann et al. (2005)) are provided in Table 3.

Adverb/ Connective	*thus, therefore, together, recently, in summary*
Determiner/ Pronoun	*it, this, these, we/our*
Adverb/ Adjective	*previous, future, better*
Noun phrase	***data, report, study*; method or reference**
Modal	form of *'to be', will, remain*
Adjective	*often, recently, generally*
Verb	***show, obtain, consider, view, reveal, suggest, hypothesize, indicate, believe***
Preposition	*that, to*

Table 3: Values of Parts-of-Speech for Regulatory segments in Zimmermann (2005)

5 Conclusion and implementations

In summary, we have presented a taxonomy of knowledge assessment and attribution and a set of linguistic cues based on a literature overview of from various fields. A small corpus study indicated that the system is simple to use, yet complex enough to cover the many different ways in which biologists attribute knowledge statements. We find that the majority of cases of epistemic evaluation in biological text is instantiated by regulatory segments governed by a reporting verb, prototypically of the form: '*These results suggest'*.

To see if this correlation to epistemic evaluation holds at larger volumes, we plan to try out the above structure in an NLP environment. To begin this, we are examining the case where Value = 2/3 and Source = (I)A: in other words, the author posits a claim. These clauses constitute a specific subset of Propositional Content, which we are calling 'Claimed Knowledge Updates' (Sándor, Á. and de Waard, A., 2012). We are exploring whether an automated syntactic parsing system, combined with a specific subset of reporting verbs will allow the identification of such authorial claims of new knowledge. We plan to use this knowledge to explore what linguistic changes occur when these Claimed Knowledge Updates are cited, and study how knowledge attribution and epistemic modality erode, in the evolution from a claim to a fact.

Acknowledgments

We wish to thank Eduard Hovy for providing the insight that modality can be thought of like sentiment, and our anonymous reviewers for their constructive comments. Anita de Waard's research is supported by Elsevier Labs and a grant from the Dutch funding organization NWO, under their Casimir Programme.

References

Crompton, P. (1997) Hedging in Academic Writing: Some Theoretical Problems, Eng Spec Purposes, Vol. 16, No. 4, pp. 271-287,1997.

De Haan, F. (1999), Evidentiality and Epistemic Modality: Setting Boundaries. Southwest Journal of Linguistics 18.83-101.

De Waard, A., Pander Maat, H. (2009). Categorizing Epistemic Segment Types in Biology Research

Articles. Wkshp on Linguistic and Psycholinguistic Approaches to Text Structuring (LPTS 2009), September 21-23, 2009.

De Waard, 2012. Anita de Waard, 2012-05-23, "Overview of epistemic evaluation and cues from literature", V1, http://hdl.handle.net/1902.1/18253

Hengeveld, K. & Mackenzie, J. L. (2008), Functional Discourse Grammar: A Typologically-Based Theory of Language Structure. Oxford Univ. Press, 2008.

Hovy, E.H. (2011). Private correspondence.

Hyland, K. (1995). The Author in the Text: Hedging Scientific Writing. Hong Kong Papers In Linguistics And Language Teaching, 18 (1995).

Hyland, K. (2005). Stance and engagement: a model of interaction in academic discourse. Discourse Studies, Vol 7(2): 173–192.

Kilicoglu H., Bergler S. (2008). Recognizing speculative language in biomedical research articles: a linguistically motivated perspective. BMC Bioinformatics. 2008 Nov 19;9 Suppl 11:S10.

Kim, S-M. Hovy, E.H. (2004). Determining the Sentiment of Opinions. Proceedings of the COLING conference, Geneva, 2004.

Lakoff G. (1972). Hedges: a study in meaning criteria and the logic of fuzzy concepts. Chicago Linguistics Society Papers 1972, 8:183-228.

Latour, B., Woolgar, S. (1979). Laboratory Life: The Social Construction of Scientific Facts. Beverly Hills: Sage Publications. ISBN 0-80-390993-4.

Light M., Qiu X.Y., Srinivasan P. (2004). The language of bioscience: facts, speculations, and statements in between. BioLINK 2004: Linking Biological Literature, Ontologies and Databases 2004:17-24.

Martín-Martín, P. (2008). The Mitigation Of Scientific Claims In Research Papers: A Comparative Study. Int Jnl of English 2008 8(2): 133-152.

Medlock B., Briscoe T. (2007). Weakly supervised learning for hedge classification in scientific literature. ACL 2007:992-999.

Myers, G. (1992). 'In this paper we report': Speech acts scientific facts, Jnl of Pragmatlcs 17 (1992) 295-313

Salager-Meyer, F. (1994), Hedges and Textual Communicative Function in Medical English Written Discourse, English for Specific Purposes, Vol. 13, No. 2, PP. 149-170, 1994.

Sándor, Á. and de Waard, A (2012). Identifying Claimed Knowledge Updates in Biomedical Research Articles, Workshop on Detecting Structure in Scholarly Discourse at ACL 2012 (this workshop).

Tang, H., Tan, S., Cheng, X. (2009), A survey on sentiment detection of reviews, Expert Systems with Applications 36 (2009) 10760–10773.

Thomas, S. and Hawes, Th. P. (1994). Reporting Verbs in Medical Journal Articles, English for Specific Purposes, 1994 13(2), pp. 129-148.

Thompson P., Venturi G., McNaught J, Montemagni S, Ananiadou S. (2008). Categorising modality in biomedical texts.. LREC 2008: Building and Evaluating Resources for Biomedical Text Mining 2008.

Verstraete, J.-C. (2001). Jnl of Pragmatics 33 (2001).

Vincze, V., Szarvas, Farkas, Móra and Csirik, (2008). The BioScope corpus: biomedical texts annotated for uncertainty, negation and their scopes, BMC Bioinformatics 2008, 9 (Suppl 11):S9.

Voorhoeve P.M., le Sage C., et. al (2006). A genetic screen implicates miRNA-372 and miRNA-373 as oncogenes in testicular germ cell tumors. *Cell.* 2006 Mar 24;124(6):1169-81.

Wilson, T. and Wiebe, J., (2003), Annotating Opinions in the World Press, 2003, SigDAIL

Wilbur W.J., Rzhetsky A, Shatkay H (2006). New directions in biomedical text annotations: definitions, guidelines and corpus construction. BMC Bioinformatics 2006, 7:356.

Zimmermann,N., Colyer, JL, Koch, LE and Rothenberg, ME. (2005). Analysis of the CCR3 promoter reveals a regulatory region in exon 1 that binds GATA-1, BMC Immunology 2005, 6:7-7.

Appendix:

Table A1: Example of markup with epistemic evaluation/knowledge attribution types and markers from Zimmermann (2005) – for table headers see caption.

Clause	Value	Basis	Source	Modal	Adv/ Adj	Refs	RV?	Ruled by RV?
DNase I hypersensitivity indicated that	2	D	IA				1	
a region consistent with exon 1 is active in CCR3 transcription.	2	D	IA					1
Together with our previous data showing that	3	D	A				1	
untranslated exon 1 has an important role in CCR3 transcription [27],	3	D	N		1	1		1
we hypothesized that	1	R	A				1	
nuclear proteins bind to exon 1,	2	D	IA					1
and in turn regulate the transcription of CCR3.	2	D	IA					1
In order to test this hypothesis,							1	
a double-stranded oligonucleotide probe that corresponds to bp +10 to +60 of the CCR3 gene was prepared,	3	0	NN					
referred to as E1-FL (exon 1- full length, Figure 2A).	3	D	A			1	1	
This is the exact sequence	3	D	N					
that was deleted in the CCR3(-exon1).pGL3 plasmid	3	D	N					
that demonstrated decreased activity	3	D	N				1	
compared to the full length 1.6 kb construct [27].	3	D	N			1	1	1
Nuclear extracts from AML14.3D10 cells were incubated with the probe								
and resolved on a polyacrylamide gel.								
Two bands were visible (Figure 2B).	3	D	IA			1	1	
The upper band was eliminated	3	D	IA				1	
when 150x molar excess of the unlabelled probe was used (CC: E1-FL in Figure Figure2B),2B),						1		
indicating that	2	D	IA				1	
this is the specific band.	2	D	IA					1
The specific band was eliminated with E1-B and E1-C cold competitors	3	D	IA				1	
indicating that	2	D	IA				1	
the factor binds in the region between +25 and +60 (Figure 2B).	2	D	IA			1		1
In summary, these data indicate	2	D	IA				1	
the presence of proteins in the nuclei of AML14.3D10 cells that bind to CCR3 exon 1 between bp 25 and 60.	2	D	IA					1

'Modal' = containing a modal auxiliary verb; 'Refs' = containing a reference; 'Adverb/Adj' = containing a qualifying adverb or adjective; 'RV' = Reporting verb; 'Ruled by RV' = in a subclause ruled by a matrix clause containing a reporting verb.

Table A2: Correlation between modality type (rows) and modality cues (columns) for two full-text papers

Value	Basis	Source	Modal Aux	Reporting Verb	Ruled by RV	Adverbs/ Adjectives	References	None	*Total*
3	0	0						8	*8*
3	0	IA		5	2	2			*9*
3	0	N		8	5	2	8	2	*25*
3	0	NN	1	2	2			12	*17*
3	D	A		20	1		16	2	*39*
3	D	IA		33	6	1	9	17	*62*
3	D	N		7	7	1	8	6	*29*
3	D	NN		3					*3*
3	R	IA		2	1	1			*4*
3	R	NN		1					*1*
Total value = 3			*1 (0.5%)*	*81 (40%)*	*24 (12%)*	*7 (4%)*	*41 (20%)*	*47 (24%)*	*201(100%)*
2	0	N			1		1		*2*
2	0	NN		1	1				*2*
2	D	0			1				*1*
2	D	A		1					*1*
2	D	IA		22	17		1		*40*
2	D	NN		1					*1*
2	R	0			2	1	1		*4*
2	R	IA		2			1		*3*
2	R	N		1	1				*2*
2	R	NN		1					*1*
Total Value = 2			*0*	*29 (51%)*	*23 (40%)*	*1 (2%)*	*4(7%)*	*0*	*57(100%)*
1	0	0			1				*1*
1	0	NN	1	1	1		1		*4*
1	D	IA	5	5	3	1			*14*
1	R	A	2	2	5				*9*
1	R	IA	1	1					*2*
1	R	NN		2	1				*3*
Total Value = 1			*9(27%)*	*11(33%)*	*11(33%)*	*1(3%)*	*1(3%)*	*0*	*33(100%)*
0	0	0		6	1				*7*
0	0	N		1			1		*2*
0	D	0			1				*1*
0	D	N			1				*1*
0	D	NN				1			*1*
0	R	A		1					*1*
0	R	IA		1					*1*
Total Value = 0			*0*	*9 (64%)*	*3 (21%)*	*1(7%)*	*1(7%)*	*0*	*14(100%)*
Total No Modality			**0**	**16**	**3**	**0**	**3**	**22**	***44***
Overall Total			*10 (2%)*	*146(23%)*	*64(10%)*	*10(2%)*	*50(8%)*	*69(11%)*	*640(100%)*

Author Index